FISH
AND SHELLFISH

By George Lassalle
Illustrated by Alan Cracknell

PANTHEON BOOKS • NEW YORK

To two favorite hostesses,
Margaret Hoffenberg and Pru Seymour

FIRST AMERICAN EDITION

Text Copyright © 1986 by Caroline Lassalle
Illustrations Copyright © 1986 by Walker Books, Ltd.

All rights reserved under International and Pan-American
Copyright Conventions. Published in the United States by
Pantheon Books, a division of Random House, Inc.,
New York, and simultaneously in Canada by Random House of Canada
Limited, Toronto.
Originally published in Great Britain by
Walker Books, Ltd., London, in 1986.

Library of Congress Cataloging-in-Publication Data

Lassalle, George.
Fish and shellfish.
(A Pantheon classic cookbook)
Originally published: London:
Walker Books, 1986.
Includes index.
1. Cookery (Fish) 2. Cookery (Seafood)
I. Title. II. Series.
TX747.L29 1987 641.6'92 86-30508
ISBN 0-394-56168-6

Printed in Italy

CONTENTS

INTRODUCTION

For over three years now I have been haunted by a short newspaper report to the effect that a whole generation of cooks under the age of thirty was largely unfamiliar with fresh fish. I drew little comfort from a BBC World Service program, a regular feature dealing with the merchant navy, paradoxically implying that we no longer have one, that our fishing industry hardly exists, and that we no longer have two oceangoing trawlers to rub together. Then, suddenly last summer, when I began to consider the writing of this book, *Fish and Shellfish*, I received a fascinating newsletter from which I feel impelled, with the author's kind permission, to quote the following paragraphs:

"Island race we may be but we eat very little fish. 5 oz. per person per week is the (terribly low) figure fish authorities arrive at; and if only fresh fish, not frozen, is considered, our average consumption dwindles much more alarmingly to 1 lb. *per household* every 5 weeks. How has this happened and what can we do about it? The more one thinks about it the more lunatic it seems that the harvest of the seas with which we are surrounded, a food which is so rich in nutritional value, containing a high percentage of protein and a high proportion of *unsaturated* fat, is relatively speaking so greatly undervalued . . .

"If none of us does anything one sees a situation in just a few years' time in which fresh fish is virtually unobtainable and our children, though familiar with crab sticks, find it almost inconceivable that one could eat a crab." (David Mellor, *Cook's Commentary*, no. 3, summer 1985.)

Embedded in all statistics, others are concealed, and, from the lamentable figures quoted above, the fact emerges that, for several years, vast numbers of the population have eaten no fish at all. A sad predicament for young families deprived of a source of delicious nourishment. Grim tidings for a fish fanatic such as myself, whose desire has, for decades, been to assist in promoting a healthy fish-eating and home fish-cooking habit in the nation.

How has this melancholy situation come about? Most authorities blame it chiefly on a rapid decline in "retail outlets," that valuable and seriously threatened species, the neighborhood fishmonger, who seems, at first sight unaccountably, to have lost the support of an increasingly junk-food-consuming and carnivorous public. But the fishmonger's eventual fate might long ago have been foreseen when the first hamburger franchise came to Britain, and that fate was sealed when a recent pope (successor of Saint Peter the fisherman!) dealt him a mortal blow by abolishing the willingly accepted, health-giving and economically sensible Roman Catholic discipline of fish on Friday.

In this doom-laden atmosphere, to sit down and compose a new fish cookery book seemed to call for blind faith and an almost missionary zeal. Although the simple one-line message such a book should carry was immediately clear to me—"Fish is good for you, and fun to cook"—I reflected that the written word seemed to have lost its power to reach those most in need of instruction. Never before has there been so much space devoted to fine cookery writing. In the national press, the glossies, the important weeklies, splendid recipes of all kinds appear, and fish gets perhaps more than its fair share of coverage. But it would seem that the bulk of this splendid preachment is to the converted. I applaud the cult for fish that has been created by all this expert writing, particularly among young, sophisticated enthusiasts consuming their sashimi, gravlax, and seviche. Happily, the publisher has recognized the need to encourage people to buy more fish. Look at the lavish displays of the beautiful creatures in the larger stores; there is an abundance to choose from. More fish is sold in controlled-atmosphere packaging too, which keeps it fresh for a longer time. I hope that this new wealth of fish and the ideas in this book will persuade more people to try it.

George Lassalle

THE VARIETY OF FISH

For the home cook, quite apart from its manifest nutritional advantages, fish has the additional attraction, with its great variety of species, textures, and flavors, of offering a vastly wide choice which cannot be matched by even the most competitive butcher, however talented and creative he is with his sharp sculpting knives, his string and his larding needle. Fish, moreover, are beautiful. Words can do little to convey the beauty of these triumphs of aquanautical design, and the writer must content himself with ritually intoning the litany of their noble names.

Here, however, the artist can step in to do justice to the scene: the brilliant impression of a fishmonger surrounded by his tempting wares is a tribute to his stock, which would nowadays include most of the fish that at one time were only seasonably available, such as salmon and trout, and certain shellfish and crustacea. Thanks to Scottish enterprise the oyster, too, I hear with joy, may soon be in all-the-year-round supply. Many other fish that it would have surprised the citizen of twenty-five years ago to find at his fishmonger's are now available. Some have been demanded by British tourists, back from Mediterranean holidays, some by fish-loving immigrants.

Now we come to the naming of names with which we should become intimately familiar:

Anchovy, angelfish, bass, bloater, bonito, bream, brill, carp, cod, conger, dab, dogfish, eel, flounder, garfish, gurnard, haddock, hake, halibut, herring, John Dory, ling, mackerel, monkfish, mullet (gray and red), perch, pilchard, pollock, salmon, salmon trout, sardine, shad, skate, sole (Dover and lemon), sprat, tope, trout (river), tuna, turbot, and whiting.

The list covers practically all fish—with the exception, for the moment, of shellfish and cephalopods—with which we are likely to have to deal. For the fish cook's convenience (not, I hasten to add, the zoologist's), they can be divided into four separate types, as the table opposite shows.

NONOILY FISH

FIRM	SOFT
Angelfish	Cod
Bass	Dab
Bream	Flounder
Brill	Haddock
Carp	Ling
Conger	Pollock
Dogfish	Sole (lemon)
Garfish	Whiting
Hake	
Halibut	
John Dory	
Monkfish	
Mullet (gray and red)	
Perch	
Skate	
Sole (Dover)	
Tope	
Turbot	

OIL-RICH FISH

FIRM	SOFT
Bonito	Anchovy
Eel	Bloater
Gurnard	Herring
Mackerel	Pilchard
Salmon	Sardine
Salmon Trout	Sprat
Shad	
Trout (river)	
Tuna	

We shall therefore approach fish in terms of these four types: nonoily and firm; oil-rich and firm; nonoily and soft; oil-rich and soft.

Note: the word *oily* has dreadful echoes of the garage, the highway, tractor-trailer trucks. *Oil-rich,* too, has unwelcome overtones, suggesting fishy Texans or secret hoards of cholesterol, which is the opposite of the case. In a former book, as if the fish might overhear me and be offended, I avoided the use of the word *soft,* using the term *less firm* to describe fish that, owing to the delicacy of their texture, are quicker-cooking and more easily ruined by overcooking than are firm fish. However, we should not look on the terms *oily* or *soft* as being in any way derogatory.

The differing characteristics of the fish naturally influence the choice of cooking method, the time taken to cook the fish, the sauces suitable for dressing them, and the amount of fish to provide per portion. Most smoked fish are of the oil-rich type, haddock being a miraculous and happy exception. (Cod, another nonoily fish, does not smoke nearly so successfully.)

Choice of cooking method

For all oil-rich fish, broiling is the method *par excellence.* The large poached salmon, served with an oil-rich mayonnaise or a butter-opulent hollandaise, however delicious, is an absurdity in modern dietetic terms. For nonoily fish, no restriction can be put on the method of cooking. It is good grilled, perhaps better poached, and excellent cooked *á la meunière.* Oil-rich fish, on the other hand, are not used in soups or the making of fish stocks.

Cooking times

All fish cooks quickly; soft fish cooks very quickly. Indeed, small quantities poached in a stock may very well be found to be cooked when the stock comes to the simmering point.

Suitable dressings

Herb relishes, ketchups, vinaigrette, and sauces based on purees of vegetables seem to be indicated for oil-rich fish, while for nonoily fish, all the butter-, egg-, and cream-based sauces of the great French cooking tradition can be called upon.

Size of portions
Although some professional chefs recommend that a whole fish weighing from 5 to 7 ounces should suffice for one person, to me this suggests the shrewd administrator rather than the bonhomous cook, for it would take fine surgery, indeed, at the table to extract more than half the weight from the whole fish.

My own view is that the minimum weight of whole fish for one person should be something over 8 ounces, to provide 6 ounces of fillet. We can then accept this quantity as a healthy average minimum portion per person, as a main dish, accompanied by sauce, vegetables, etc. For a first or second among a number of courses, the quantity may be allowed to sink as low as 2½ to 3 ounces. But this is not the whole story.

The quality and texture of the fish often influence the norm, for oil-rich fish are more "filling." For example, 5 ounces of salmon will be as satisfying as 7 ounces of flounder. These variations in the "filling" potential of fish types have to be taken into account. The individual quirks of human metabolisms make it impossible to define precisely the meanings of the terms *filling* and *satisfying*.

NOTES FOR FISH COOKS
Frozen fish
My experience with frozen fish is not extensive, though I have nothing against its use. I would not presume to contradict any instructions given by the makers on their packages, and my advice is to follow them to the letter. If the result displeases, then complain at once. My own limited practice is to defrost frozen fish completely in the refrigerator before attempting to cook it, bearing in mind that, although thawed out, it may still be very cold deep inside and either should be allowed to reach room temperature in the kitchen or should have allowance made in its cooking time.

Of "boil in the bag," ready-sauced items, I have nothing to say except that they are a direct disincentive to home cooking.

Preparation of fish
Normally, if you buy a fish whole, the fishmonger will, at your request, scale, decapitate, clean, fillet, and skin the fish so that it is ready to cook.

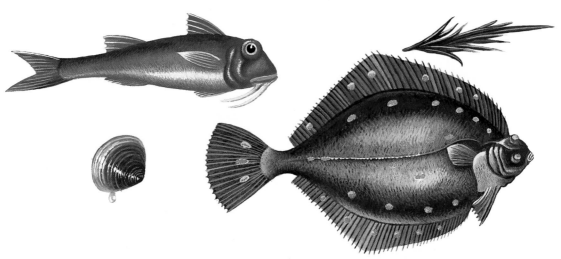

Cooking times

This is a subject that makes cowards of us all. Some of the greatest cookery writers have taken refuge behind the evasive phrase, such as "cook until it is done enough" or, more succinctly, "nicely done" or, with an abrupt abdication of all responsibility, "until the fish is cooked." Sadly enough, when modern writers have stood their ground and come out boldly with precise poaching or broiling times for given weights or thicknesses of fish, they have on occasion been grotesquely wide of the mark.

My own, no-less-fallible estimates of poaching and broiling times are given under the appropriate method headings later in this book. Otherwise, timings for given weights and thicknesses of fish are included in the various recipes.

Butter and margarine

In the making of savory or compound butters (p. 18) home cooks are naturally welcome to use their own favorite brands of substitutes for butter.

Wine

Where wine is indicated for use in stocks and sauces, this does not mean the stale remnants of bottles left over from week-old parties. Open a new bottle as if you were going to have a glass of wine yourself (and why not do so?).

On the subject of wine to be drunk with fish, I drink both red and white with equal fervor, with a bias toward red in the case of oil-rich fish such as salmon trout and tuna.

"Finely chopped"

A personal note, this. I should perhaps apologize in advance for using in my recipes those antique phrases *finely chopped*, or *finely ground*, and *pounded into a smooth paste*, which, with all the splendid mechanized aids available to the modern home cook, may appear very much out of date. Nevertheless, there must still be kitchens here and there about the country which are not so well equipped.

In fact, I confess that fine chopping and pounding and slicing are some of the many joys I find in the recreation of cookery. These are, if you like, my form of jogging and push-ups, and keep me fit. They are marvelous exercise, especially in preserving the muscles of the arms, shoulders and chest from that "withering on the branch" effect that is so often seen as age

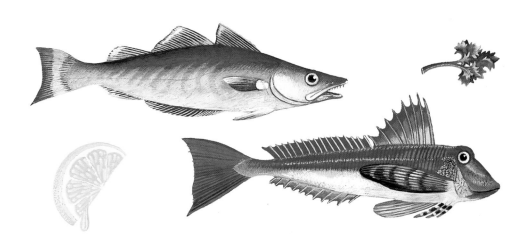

advances. Moreover, if one's chopping board is placed at a level that enables one to sit down to the task, then all the muscles of the lower body are also brought into play by the practice of trotting on the spot in time with the chopping process.

KITCHEN UTENSILS

Apart from the normal equipment of household kitchens, there are few special requirements for cooking fish. Some may seem insignificant, but my own short list of the essentials is as follows:

Implements

You will need implements for lifting or turning fish without breaking them, such as broad palette knives, flat-bladed tongs, and slotted spatulas of generous breadth. For broiling over charcoal, an implement made of strong wire that looks like two very old-fashioned tennis rackets hinged at the top and that grips four or five fish firmly is most welcome.

Larger items

I recommend an unusually large frying pan. I happen to possess one 20 inches by 9 inches of almost oval shape. This enables me to cook fillets or steaks of fish for six people at the same time and allows me to eat with my guests instead of staying at the stove and cooking *en série*. It is also a splendid pan for cooking *à la meunière* dishes.

Fish kettles and turbotières are very expensive items, but useful if you cook fish frequently. In a small kettle you can poach a sizable whole round fish, such as bass, bream, a whole large monkfish tail, larger sections of conger, and so on. A turbotière is useful not only for cooking the large whole flat fish but also for poaching a quantity of thick steaks and fillets of all kinds.

A large chafing dish fitted with a strainer enables cooked fish to be kept hot, without further cooking, while a sauce is completed.

A bain-marie is a wide, shallow "bath" (large pan) to contain hot water, in which finished sauces or those awaiting completion can be stood to keep hot.

Miscellanea

Some good, sharp small knives; one long, very sharp knife, the tip of which can be held down on the chopping board by two fingers of one hand while the other hand moves it around in an arc as it chops herbs and vegetables; sieves of different sizes and gauges; a scale that will register very small quantities; a clock; and, I

14

almost forgot to mention, an asparagus kettle, which I have always found invaluable for making fish soups.

Crockery
Earthenware or porcelain dishes of various sizes; terrines; molds for shaping pâtés, mousses, and so on; soufflé dishes; wide, shallow baking dishes for cooking large fish; a large platter on which to display a whole fish.

SOME USEFUL COOKING TERMS

Beurre manié
Equal quantities of butter and flour, worked together to a paste. It is added to the liquid in which food has been poached to thicken and bind it and make a sauce.

Bouquet garni
A bundle of herbs, usually thyme, parsley, and bay leaf, tied with string, used for flavoring stocks and court bouillons.

Court bouillon
A stock composed of water with wine or vinegar and savory herbs and vegetables, in which fish is to be poached.

Fumet
A concentrated essence of fish and seasonings, resulting from the reduction by boiling of strong fish stock from, say 4 cups to 1 cup. It is used for enhancing sauces and soups. A fumet usually sets into a jelly when cold.

Marinade
A liquid usually containing vinegar, wine, herbs, and spices, in which, prior to cooking, fish is laid to acquire flavor. Also a mild pickling mixture for sousing herring or mackerel.

Panada
A dough used in making fish quenelles (see p. 88).

Roux
A thickening agent in the making of sauces. It is a mixture of flour and butter in roughly equal quantities, cooked together as the basis for most sauces needing body (e.g., béchamel).

METHODS OF COOKING
I give recipes for most of the fish likely to be found today at a good fish counter, and I have suggested sauces for each one. In every case, however, you may decide whether to make the sauce suggested or whether to choose instead to put together—it takes only minutes—a relish or savory butter to accompany the dish.

1

THE DRESSING OF FISH

I t is often with the approach to sauce making that the aspiring fish cook's courage begins to fail as he or she contemplates the seeming vastness and illusory complexities of the subject. The ensuing pages will, I hope, completely dispel such misconceptions.

It is a critical psychological moment for the home cook. She or he has reached the point where cooking can continue to be a boring chore or it can become a happy form of mental recreation: devising and making sauces is an absorbing craft.

I recommend studying the relishes and savory butters that follow. They are extremely simple and enable you to dress a wide range of fish at short notice.

They are followed by the five foundation sauces—the basics of French cooking.

RELISHES

CONDIMENTS, KETCHUPS, AND BUTTERS
Everyone who has ever been in a fried-fish shop knows what a relish is. It is what one hopes is in those choked-up bottles on the tables. It is also what everyone has with roast lamb; namely, mint sauce. It is a true relish, mint sauce, put together with mint, vinegar, water and sugar, salt, pepper perhaps. But you never find two mint sauces exactly the same. Some like it thick with mint and strong with vinegar; some like it thin in both these ingredients, with plenty of sugar; some even like it hot.

The example of mint sauce and its permutations enables me to make an important point, as I am about to propose some eighty relishes, none of which should take longer than a few minutes to make. The contents can be varied in their relative quantities as the cook desires; the quantities I give merely reflect my own taste. Each cook will discover which are to be his or her favorites. For assembling relishes, all the herbs, spices, and aromatic vegetables are available to the cook. It is a limitless field.

BASIC CONSTANTS

⅓ cup wine vinegar

⅓ cup water

1 small anchovy fillet, finely pounded

1 small onion, finely chopped

juice of ½ lemon

½ teaspoon sugar

½ teaspoon finely ground black pepper

FLAVORING INGREDIENTS

The flavor chosen should dominate in the relish; use in the quantities given:

1 teaspoon ground ginger

1 teaspoon creamed horseradish

1 teaspoon ground green peppercorns

1 teaspoon crushed garlic

1 teaspoon prepared mustard

1 teaspoon ground cumin

2 teaspoons puree of celery

2 teaspoons puree of fennel

2 teaspoons finely chopped tarragon

2 teaspoons finely chopped basil

2 teaspoons puree of capers

1 tablespoon puree of raw mushrooms

1 tablespoon puree of sweet peppers

1 tablespoon puree of gherkins

1 tablespoon puree of tomato

2 teaspoons puree of black olives

HERBS

These herbs have a special affinity with fish, and one of them should always be present in a relish, in the quantites given:

2 teaspoons finely chopped parsley

2 teaspoons finely chopped chervil

2 teaspoons finely chopped thyme

2 teaspoons finely chopped dill

1 teaspoon ground bay leaf

Method

Select a flavoring ingredient and an herb from the lists opposite and combine them together well with the basic constants. Allow the mixture to stand for an hour before using.

These relishes are particularly effective with all oil-rich fish. They have the full status of sauces, and I am never reluctant to serve them. I only wish that they were more frequently used in restaurants.

For nonoily fish, the addition of 2 tablespoons olive oil is an improvement, though this is not necessary. Without the olive oil, the relishes can be turned into hot butter sauces. Simply heat the relish and beat into it 4 tablespoons butter. Keep hot, but do not let it boil.

BUTTERS: SAVORY AND COMPOUND

As with the relishes, here again we have a plentiful supply of varied and delicious miniature sauces that can be easily made in a matter of minutes. There are at least fifty of these butters recorded in the classic canon, but this still leaves plenty of room for experiment and improvisation.

Select an herb, spice, or aromatic from the flavoring ingredients opposite. The rules are few and simple:

The proportion to be maintained is ¼ pound butter to the given amount of each flavoring ingredient or herb in the lists.

In addition to your selected flavoring ingredient, there should always be included parsley, one member of the onion family (chives, shallots, scallions, etc.), a drop or two of lemon juice, and a pinch each of salt and finely ground black pepper.

Use these butters also to make croutons for cocktail parties and buffets. Serve them with potatoes in their jackets, and use them to season many other vegetables. They are truly all-purpose miniature sauces.

GARLIC BUTTER

This is a pattern recipe.

SERVES 4 OR 5

¼ pound unsalted butter, softened	1 teaspoon crushed garlic
2 teaspoons finely chopped parsley	2 drops lemon juice
2 teaspoons finely chopped chives	pinch each of salt and finely ground black pepper

Simply blend the butter with all the other ingredients and put in the refrigerator to harden until required for use. This amount of butter will anoint sufficient fish for 4 or 5 people. It is excellent for use with all kinds of fish, especially broiled or poached fillets and steaks of nonoily fish and with fish fried *à la meunière*.

CREAM SAUCE

Savory butters can also be used in making quick cream sauces.

MAKES ¾ cup

¼ pound savory butter (p. 18)	scant ⅔ cup heavy cream

Put the savory butter into a saucepan to melt over low heat. When hot, pour in the cream. Stir briskly as it comes to the simmering point. Simmer for a short minute. Strain through a sieve and keep warm. If you prefer a thinner sauce, use light cream.

THE FOUNDATION SAUCES

These five sauces, together with the relishes and butters given earlier, provide the home cook with all the tools necessary for the construction of a personal style of haute cuisine.

Béchamel and velouté are flour-based sauces, the former made with milk, the latter with stock. Hollandaise and mayonnaise are suspensions in egg yolk of butter and oil respectively. Vinaigrette is a careful balance of oil, vinegar, salt, and pepper, which can be embellished with herbs, mustard or shallots.

BÉCHAMEL SAUCE

Béchamel, or white sauce, is prolific and is the basis for many of the best sauces in the French classic repertoire. Sauces derived from béchamel and the other foundation sauces that follow will appear in the recipes.

MAKES 2½ cups SAUCE

3 tablespoons butter	a spring each of parsley and thyme, and a bay leaf
3 tablespoons flour	
3½ cups milk, heated together with 1 small onion, finely chopped	¼ teaspoon salt
	¼ teaspoon ground black pepper

Melt the butter in a saucepan over low heat. Add the flour and mix together well to form a paste; cook for about 1 minute. Remove from the stove and gradually add the hot milk with the onion and other ingredients, stirring vigorously to effect a homogenous blending of paste and milk. Return to the stove and keep stirring as the sauce simmers gently for 20 minutes. Remove from the heat and allow to cool, stirring occasionally. Strain through a sieve.

Note: almost any savory butter added to a béchamel, made as above, and improved with cream produces an excellent sauce in its own right.

FISH VELOUTÉ

This is the basis for any number of soups and sauces for fish of all kinds; its quality and fine flavor will very much depend on the nature of the fish stock with which it is made. Here I use a good standard stock, but it must not be forgotten that every herb, spice, and aromatic vegetable is available to vary its flavor, strength, and style and so radically affect the end result. No trimmings of oil-rich fish should ever be used in making the stock for a velouté.

MAKES 2½ cups SAUCE

For the fish stock

6 ounces nonoily white fish trimmings (e.g., from flounder, sole, or whiting)

1 small carrot, grated

½ stalk celery, coarsely chopped

2 shallots, coarsely chopped

2 or 3 sprigs of parsley

1 bay leaf

½ teaspoon salt

½ teaspoon ground black pepper

For the sauce

3 tablespoons butter

3 tablespoons flour

3½ cups fish stock

Boil the fish trimmings and all the other ingredients for the stock in 3¾ cups water for 30 minutes. Allow to cool, then strain. Proceed as for béchamel sauce (p. 19), but use the fish stock in place of the seasoned milk.

HOLLANDAISE SAUCE

Egg yolks whisked with butter over low heat thicken to form an emulsion. Hollandaise is an excellent sauce in its own right and the basis for a range of egg-thickened sauces.

MAKES 1 cup SAUCE

6 ounces unsalted butter, softened

4 tablespoons wine vinegar or 2 of vinegar and 2 of lemon juice

12 peppercorns

2 egg yolks

½ teaspoon salt

Divide the butter into small pieces. Reduce the vinegar by boiling with the peppercorns to about 2 or 3 tablespoons of liquid and strain into another pan. Allow to cool a little. Then beat in the egg yolks with a whisk.

Now, over a very low heat, or in a bain-marie (p. 14) gradually beat in half the butter and the salt. When the mixture begins to thicken, add the remaining butter, a little at a time, whisking continuously until the mixture has the texture of heavy cream.

VARIATION

Any of the relishes on p. 16 may be reduced over heat to a few strained tablespoons of savory liquid and be used in place of the vinegar to produce variants of hollandaise, an infinitely variable sauce for all fish, hot or cold.

MAYONNAISE

MAKES about 2 cups

2 egg yolks

1 teaspoon powdered or
prepared mustard

2 teaspoons wine vinegar

1 teaspoon salt

½ teaspoon finely ground
black pepper

scant 2 cups olive oil

If using eggs taken from the refrigerator, allow the yolks time to reach room temperature. In a bowl, blend together the first five ingredients and stir for 1 minute. Then, drop by drop to begin with, add the olive oil. As the mixture begins to thicken, pour in the oil in a thin steady stream.

VARIATIONS

Here again, the relishes (p. 16) come in handy. Reduce the relish, by boiling, to a few tablespoons. Pour through a sieve and allow to cool.

Use 1 teaspoon concentrate in lieu of the mustard, vinegar, salt, and pepper in the above recipe, to blend into the egg yolks before adding the oil. You can thus make many subtle variants of mayonnaise.

VINAIGRETTE SAUCE

This, in all its simplicity, is the true basic vinaigrette, which makes a delicious dressing for all green and other salads and is not to be despised as an accompaniment to broiled, fried, or poached fish. In a vinaigrette, the proportion of oil to vinegar, as shown here, is three of oil to one of vinegar.

MAKES ½ cup

2 tablespoons wine
vinegar

salt and pepper

6 tablespoons olive oil

Whisk together the vinegar, salt, and pepper until thoroughly mixed. Add the oil in a steady stream, whisking as you do so. Taste for seasoning.

VARIATIONS

Any number of vinaigrettes can be made from the relishes (p. 16) by reducing the amount of vinegar in the relish recipe to 2 tablespoons and stirring into it 6 tablespoons olive oil. Eliminate the sugar from the relish, too, if you wish.

2
BROILING

This is probably the first method of cooking fish adopted by *Homo sapiens* when he gave up eating it raw. Broiling is a simple process, and the skills involved are quickly learned, but preparing and controlling a charcoal grill is a skill on its own. For cooking meat, there is nothing better, but for fish, it can present problems. It is best not to remove scales or head if you are using a charcoal grill. For a large fish make 2 or 3 diagonal incisions in the thicker part of the flesh. For small fish use a well-oiled double grill to hold them in place while you turn them over. Close attention to timing is essential. For everyday use, electric and gas grills are best.

Small fish, or thin fillets or steaks, should be put to a fierce heat. Thicker fish should be put to a moderate heat or laid at some distance from the source of heat, which then has time to penetrate to the center without overcooking or burning the outer flesh. Bear in mind that the rate of penetration of heat varies as the square of the thickness of your fish. Thus, if it takes 2 minutes to broil a thin piece of fish, then to broil a piece twice as thick will take not twice as long but four times as long. (I am grateful to be reminded of this basic law of physics by Alan Davidson, in his book *North Atlantic Seafood*.)

The following table is intended as a guide for broiling times of fully thawed fish of various thicknesses of steak or fillet that the cook will normally be called upon to deal with.

Thicknesses of fillets or steaks	Broiling times, turning over at half-time	
	Firm fish	Soft fish
½ inch	4 minutes	3 minutes
1 inch	10 minutes	8 minutes
1½ inches	12 minutes	10 minutes
2 inches	15 minutes	12 minutes

This table also applies to whole small unscored fish, measured at their thickest part.

As mentioned earlier (p. 12), if your fish is frozen, the instructions on the packet should be followed. The above table applies only to completely thawed-out fish at kitchen temperature. For larger whole scored fish, frequent watching and testing with a probe provides the only reliable method.

Make sure the grilling bars are hot and well oiled before the fish is put on them to cook.

When broiling, give full attention to what you are doing. Small fillets and slender steaks, particularly of soft fish, such as flounder, or cod, can be cooked on one side, under a fierce heat, in less than a minute. You must be ready with the fish tongs or other implement to turn the fish over at the right moment. When a time is given in a recipe, test a little before that time is up, by probing, with a thin, sharp skewer or knife, near the bone. If any pink shows, or the flesh displays no tendency to spring away from the bone, then go to the full time given and test again.

Fish may be laid in a marinade for some time prior to broiling, though this is not essential. A simple marinade, in which the fish should be turned occasionally while it waits to be cooked, is a mixture of olive oil, lemon juice or wine vinegar, bay leaf, a small chopped onion, salt, and pepper. Other, more elaborate marinades appear in the recipes which follow.

It is essential to baste the fish throughout the process of broiling. All that is needed is a little olive oil and lemon juice, salt and pepper, and a basting brush (the type with which you brush egg or milk on pastry). Small whole fish weighing 5 to 7 ounces can be dealt with as they are, without scoring or any attention other than basting. Fish weighing 8 ounces or over should be scored diagonally with a sharp knife on the side first to be put to the grill and, when turned, again scored diagonally in a direction opposite to the cuts on the other side; well basted; and again set to the heat. Judiciously carried out, this method of scoring will keep the fish intact and facilitate its removal to a serving dish when cooked. Whole fish weighing much over 1 pound should, for convenience, be cut into steaks for broiling.

BROILED MACKEREL WITH GOOSEBERRY SAUCE

Mackerel is a firm and oil-rich fish calling for sweet-and-sour sauces or relishes based on mustard, horse-radish, capers, etc. The simple gooseberry sauce exactly matches the temperament of the fish.

SERVES 4

four 8-ounce mackerel	For the sauce
For the marinade	1 pound unripe, green,
1¼ cups water	carefully pared
3 tablespoons wine	gooseberries
vinegar	1¼ cups water
3 tablespoons olive oil	**For basting**
juice of ½ lemon	the oil from the top
2 bay leaves, crushed	of the marinade
4 black peppercorns,	**For the garnish**
crushed	1 tablespoon parsley,
2 cloves, crushed	finely chopped
1 shallot, finely chopped	

One hour before you intend to cook them, lay the mackerel in a shallow dish to fit them and pour the marinade over them. The liquid may not cover them: never mind; turn them over once or twice. Meanwhile prepare the sauce by boiling the gooseberries in the water until soft and thick. Pass through a sieve or blender to get a good smooth puree. Set aside to keep hot. Remove the fish from the marinade and score each with 3 diagonal cuts. Put them under a moderate grill, cut side up, for 7 minutes, basting frequently with the top of the marinade. Remove them from the heat; turn them over carefully; and again score them diagonally (in reverse) with 3 cuts. Put them back under the grill for another 7 minutes, continuing to baste as they cook. Lay the fish in a heated serving dish and dress the gashes with the parsley. Serve the gooseberry sauce separately.

Suggested accompaniments: plain boiled new potatoes, small baked tomatoes.

Note: the marinade given here is a good general-purpose one that may be used for other dishes. If you decide not to use it, then baste the fish as they are broiling with a mixture of olive oil and lemon juice. Marinades are refinements and not compulsory.

BROILED GRAY MULLET WITH BERCY SAUCE

The gray mullet is the antithesis of the mackerel, being less firm of flesh and not oil-rich. A beautiful fish, aquatically streamlined, it has no very pronounced individual flavor, which invites a rich wine sauce or a simple one, as here.

SERVES 4

four 8-ounce gray mullet	1 tablespoon finely chopped parsley
For the sauce	
2 tablespoons finely chopped shallot	**For basting**
scant ⅔ cup dry white wine	2 tablespoons olive oil
	juice of 1 lemon
scant 2 cups fish velouté (p. 20)	1 teaspoon grated onion
	a good pinch of ground black pepper
4 tablespoons butter	a good pinch of salt

Make the sauce before the broiling begins. Cook the chopped shallot in the wine until the wine is reduced by half. Then stir in the velouté. Heat through and finish by stirring in the butter and the parsley. Keep warm while cooking the fish.

As in the recipe for mackerel (p. 24), score each mullet with 3 diagonal cuts on the side to be put first to the grill. Brush them well with the basting mixture and put under a moderate grill for 7 minutes, basting frequently.

Turn the fish over and repeat the scoring process. Return to the grill and cook for 7 minutes more. Baste as necessary. Remove to a hot serving dish and, using a teaspoon, fill the cuts with a little of the sauce, the bulk of which should be served separately. Serve with mashed potatoes and a very well drained puree of spinach.

BROILED SWORDFISH WITH BLACK BUTTER

This comparative newcomer to the British market is a fine firm fish, discreetly oil-rich, not as filling as tuna. It is good broiled, simply brushed over with lemon juice. Overcooked it can turn to cotton wool. With black butter, a simple sauce which should be much more widely used, it is truly a gastronomic experience.

SERVES 5–6

5–6 swordfish steaks of ½-inch thickness	scant ⅔ cup wine vinegar
For basting	juice of 1 lemon
2 tablespoons olive oil	1 tablespoon capers, finely chopped
juice of ½ lemon	
For the black butter	
¼ pound salted butter	

Cut the fish steaks in half so that you have semicircular segments. Seven minutes' broiling on each side under a moderate heat, basted with the oil-and-lemon-juice mixture, should see them well enough done. Remove them to a hot serving dish.

Now put the butter to melt over a low heat in a heavy frying pan. Watch as the butter turns, in rapid stages, from *café au lait* color to a deeper and deeper brown, until it is just about to burn. At this critical moment, slip in, down the side of the pan, the mixture of vinegar, lemon, and chopped capers. There will be a great sizzling and some smoke as the cold liquid meets the sizzling butter and you stir all around for a few seconds. Distribute the sauce, piping hot, over the hot steaks and serve.

This is an invaluable quick sauce: only half a minute from the moment your butter has melted in the pan. It should be used with all kinds of white fish fillets and steaks, as well as oil-rich fish. Definitely a sauce to remember.

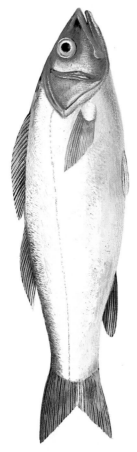

BROILED SEA BASS WITH HOLLANDAISE SAUCE

When mature, a whole sea bass extends nearly a yard in length. Firm steaks, 1 inch thick, will weigh a little over ½ pound each. So 2 pounds of this fine, solid nonoily fish, which is free of small bones, should be ample for 6 people when served with butter-rich hollandaise sauce and a supporting garnish or two. Small bass are splendid stuffed and baked or braised in the oven. They also broil well, laid on a bed of fennel to create a fine fragrance in the kitchen.

SERVES 6

2 pounds of 1-inch-thick steaks of sea bass

For basting

4 tablespoons butter, melted

juice of ½ lemon

For the garnish

2 tablespoons finely chopped parsley, mixed

with 2 teaspoons finely chopped celery

a good pinch of ground black pepper

a good pinch of salt

For the sauce

see p. 20

The sauce, and any other items for the dish, such as garnishes and vegetables, should be completed before the broiling begins. The sauce, which should not be kept waiting too long, should be stood in a bain-marie (p. 14) and whisked from time to time as the broiling proceeds.

Brush the steaks with the melted butter and lemon juice, put them to a moderate grill, and cook for 9 minutes on each side, basting well every 3 minutes. Remove to a hot serving dish. Sprinkle with the garnish. Take to the table; remove the skin; dissect and distribute judiciously. Serve the sauce separately.

Suggested accompaniment: tomatoes and/or zucchini, stuffed with cumin-spiced rice.

MONKFISH KEBABS

This is properly a recipe for a charcoal grill and an outdoor party, but it can just as easily be cooked on a normal household gas or electric broiler.

SERVES 6

2 pounds monkfish tail, cut into pieces weighing roughly 1 ounce each

For the marinade

4 cloves garlic, crushed and pounded

2 teaspoons ground ginger

2 anchovy fillets, pounded

1¼ cups water

1¼ cups white wine

3 tablespoons wine vinegar

juice of 1 lemon

bouquet garni of sprigs of thyme, parsley, bay leaf

1 tablespoon ground black pepper

1 teaspoon sugar

¼ teaspoon cayenne pepper

For the skewers

1 large carrot, cut into ¼-inch-thick rounds

¼ pound fennel bulb, very thinly sliced

1 small red pepper, deseeded, cut into 1-inch squares

1 small green pepper, deseeded, cut into 1-inch squares

12 mushrooms, halved

¼ pound celeriac, very thinly sliced

Assemble the marinade first, so that its ingredients have time to blend while the kebab skewers are being prepared. The skewers should also be assembled well before cooking time, because they should remain in the marinade for at least an hour before they are broiled.

Take 6 long skewers and load each one with the ingredients in the following order: a round of carrot, as a "stopper," then a slice of fennel bulb, a square of pepper, a mushroom half, a slice of celeriac, a piece of monkfish. Repeat this succession 3 more times,

excluding the carrot, of which a round should only be used again as a "stopper" at the sharp end of the skewer. Lay the skewers in the marinade for an hour or more, turning them frequently so that they become thoroughly impregnated with the rich flavors. If you don't have a suitable dish in which to marinate the kebabs, you can marinate the cut ingredients and thread them onto skewers just before broiling.

Put the skewers on a moderately hot grill for 2 minutes. Then give each skewer a quarter turn, clockwise, and broil for 2 minutes more. Repeat this process twice more (8 minutes in all). Baste frequently. Now raise the temperature of the grill and repeat the turning process, but this time at only 1-minute intervals. Total broiling time is 12 minutes, throughout which basting with the marinade should be continuous. Serve the skewers on a bed of plain boiled rice.

This recipe sounds complicated, but once the ingredients are to hand, the preparation time is not so very lengthy. Not for every day perhaps, but a recipe that's fun to follow as well as being quite delicious to consume, with a good strong wine.

VARIATION

Use dogfish or angel shark in place of monkfish.

27

3
POACHING

Poaching is cooking by total immersion in a vegetable and herb stock, or court bouillon, which is heated to the simmering point, but never allowed to boil. Small fish and fillets (4 to 6 ounces) will be found to be almost cooked as the court bouillon comes to the simmering point. Fish weighing from 7 ounces to 1 pound will be cooked in 2–5 minutes, depending on whether the fish is in the soft or firm category. Thereafter, the following table is as reliable as most.

Weights of fish	Firm fish	Soft fish
1 pound	6 minutes	5 minutes
1½ pound	7 minutes	6 minutes
2¼ inch	10 minutes	8 minutes
4½ pound	14 minutes	10 minutes
6¾ pound	18 minutes	15 minutes
9 pound	28 minutes	20 minutes

COURT BOUILLON

Here is a recipe for a fragrant court bouillon, adaptable to oil-rich and nonoily fish. The amount given here should be enough to poach most round and fat fish in a small pan. For cooking very big fish in a fish kettle or turbotière, more will be needed.

MAKES 2½ quarts

3 quarts water

2 carrots, shredded

2 stalks celery, chopped

4 shallots, chopped

the white of 2 leeks, chopped

2 good sprigs of thyme

2 teaspoons chopped tarragon

2 bay leaves

5 or 6 sprigs of parsley

12 black peppercorns, crushed

6 tablespoons wine vinegar

For nonoily fish: eliminate the vinegar, add the juice of a lemon, scant ⅔ cup of white wine, and 1 teaspoon salt.

Boil the ingredients briskly in the water for 20 minutes. Reduce heat and allow to simmer for 20 minutes more. Set aside to cool; then strain through a sieve.

Note: with the addition of 5 ounces of the bones of nonoily fish, flounder trimmings, and, say, a small whiting, this court bouillon becomes a **rich fish stock**. When further enriched by the juices of fish poached in it, and then reduced by steady boiling to half, it becomes a **concentrated fish stock**, or **fumet**, invaluable for the making of sumptuous velouté sauces (p. 20) and soups (chapter 10).

SKATE WITH POULETTE SAUCE AU CITRON

A rare occasion this, when skate is divorced from the black butter sauce (p. 25) with which it also goes so well.

SERVES 4

four 7-ounce wings of skate (if fillets are free of cartilaginous bone, 6 ounce per person is enough)	*2 tablespoons butter*
	a good pinch of grated nutmeg
For the sauce	*juice of 2 lemons*
1 medium onion, finely chopped	*2 tablespoons finely chopped parsley*
1¼ cups white wine	*salt and black pepper to taste*
scant 2 cups fish velouté (p. 20), warmed	**For poaching**
2 egg yolks	*court bouillon for nonoily fish (p. 28)*

The sauce should be made before cooking of the fish is begun. The ingredients given above are sufficient for approximately 2 cups of sauce.

Cook the onion with the wine until the wine is reduced to a few tablespoons. Strain into the warm velouté, mixing together well. Now beat the egg yolks with 3 tablespoons of the hot but not boiling sauce; then add this egg mixture to the rest of the sauce, which must be kept hot but, from now on, not allowed to simmer or boil. Add the butter, the nutmeg, the lemon juice, stirring well. To finish, fold in 1 tablespoon of parsley, and season with salt and pepper to taste. While you are poaching the skate, keep the sauce hot in a bain-marie (p. 14), stirring from time to time.

Cover the wings of skate with court bouillon. Bring to a simmer and poach for 3 minutes. Now probe, with a skewer or sharp-pointed knife, where the thick cartilaginous bone meets the flesh. If pinkness is present, poach on for another minute. Then probe again. As soon as all pinkness has gone and the flesh begins to slip from the bone, the skate is done. Drain well and remove to a hot serving dish. Cover each wing with some of the sauce and scatter the remaining tablespoon of parsley over all. Bring the balance of the sauce to table in a bowl.

Suggested accompaniments: small, boiled carrots, buttered and browned in the oven, and mashed potatoes.

POACHED GURNARD WITH SOUBISE SAUCE

The gurnard is a firm fish, and oil-rich, albeit subtly so. The soubise, an onion sauce, is a simple one—the addition of capers is my own idea. Here again, the sauce should be cooked before poaching begins.

SERVES 4

two 1-pound gurnards

For the sauce

¼ pound unsalted butter

3 medium-size onions, finely chopped

1¼ cups béchamel sauce (p. 19)

2 tablespoons light cream

1 tablespoon capers, crushed

a sprinkle of ground black pepper and salt

For poaching

sufficient court bouillon for oil-rich fish (p. 28) to cover the fish

The ingredients for the sauce makes about 2 cups. Melt the butter in a saucepan. Add the chopped onions and cook gently, without letting the onions take color, until they are soft, transparent, and almost melting. Pass through a sieve or blender and stir into the béchamel. Add the cream. Let the sauce cook gently, stirring constantly. Just before serving, mix in the crushed capers and the pepper and salt. To electrify this sauce, and as a variant, add 1 tablespoon of the juice of a large Spanish onion.

Let the court bouillon be cool when you immerse the gurnards in it. Bring to the simmering point quickly. From this moment, 6 minutes should suffice to cook the fish. Serve them and extract the fillets from the fish at the table. This is a comparatively simple task, owing to the structure of the fish. The fish should be served alone on the plate, with its accompanying sauce; a potato, tomato, and finely sliced celeriac salad can be served separately.

JOHN DORY WITH GRIBICHE SAUCE

The "peacock of the sea," "Christ's fish" in Cyprus, "Saint Peter" in Greece and France, the John Dory is a firm, nonoily fish of exquisite flavor. A little rare in the United States, it may be available in gourmet shops with a fish department. A Dory of just over 2 pounds in weight should provide 4 excellent bone-free fillets. Ask the fishmonger to chop off the tall spines, fins, and head, saving this last for stocks and soups.

SERVES 4

1 John Dory, just over 2 pounds

For the sauce

4 yolks of hard-boiled eggs

1 teaspoon creamed horseradish

½ teaspoon salt

½ teaspoon ground black pepper

1¼ cups olive oil

2 teaspoons wine vinegar

1 teaspoon each of finely chopped parsley, gherkin, chives, and fresh tarragon

For poaching

sufficient court bouillon for nonoily fish (p. 28) to cover the fish

Blend together the egg yolks, horseradish, salt, and pepper. Add the oil very slowly until the mixture thickens and the oil is absorbed. Stir in the vinegar and fold in all the finely chopped herbs. Let the sauce warm up a little (it should be neither hot nor cold) in a bain-marie (p. 14) or on the side of the stove.

Lay the Dory in the cold court bouillon. Bring it, not too fast, to the simmering point. Simmer gently for 10 minutes. Then remove the pan from the heat and, with a sharp knife, cut down the dark, curving line which helpfully indicates the lay of the fillets within. The skin should now be rolled away to each side, exposing the fillets. Probe gently with the knife at the juncture of the fillets and the spine; if the fish is cooked, the fillet will tend to separate easily from the main bone. If the fillet still adheres to the bone, simmer for another minute and try again. Remove the fish to a dish and lift out the two exposed fillets, then the main bone, leaving the way free for the two fillets underneath to be lifted. The John Dory is one of the easiest fish to fillet. Place the fillets on four heated plates, with spoonfuls of the warm gribiche sauce on two sides and creamy-white mashed potatoes on the other two.

VARIATION

A small turbot of similar weight may be treated in exactly the same way as above. The gribiche is a sauce for all nonoily fish, firm or soft.

POACHED TURBOT WITH TARTARE SAUCE

In texture, turbot is undoubtedly the fineset white fish to be had. For flavor, my vote goes to the John Dory. However, both Dover sole and brill come very close.

SERVES 4

four 8-ounce steaks of turbot	1¼ cups mayonnaise (p. 21)
For the sauce	**For poaching**
1 teaspoon each of finely chopped chives, capers, parsley, gherkins, green olives, and red peppers	court bouillon for nonoily fish (p. 28) to cover
	For the garnish
pinch of cayenne pepper	1 small bunch of watercress, coarsely chopped
1 tablespoon olive oil	1 lemon, sliced

The sauce should be prepared before the fish is cooked. Blend together all the sauce ingredients except the mayonnaise, to form a paste. Incorporate the paste into the mayonnaise. The tartare is a delicious sauce,

piquant and deservedly popular. It goes well with almost any hot or cold fish, whether broiled, poached, as here, deep-fried, or *à la meunière*. Try it with angelfish, tope, monk, salmon, trout, Dover or lemon sole, flounder, sea bass, bream, and, as we shall see later, with shellfish of all kinds.

Put the turbot steaks into the cold court bouillon and poach them for 5 minutes; test with a sharp knife near the main bone. When cooked, lay the steaks on a warmed dish covered with the coarsely chopped watercress. Decorate with slices of lemon. Serve the sauce separately, as an accompaniment.

DOVER SOLE MORNAY

A fine dish, in which the cheese sauce blends perfectly with the firm flesh of the fish.

SERVES 4

four 6-ounce fillets of Dover sole

For the sauce

2½ cups fish velouté sauce (p. 20)

2 tablespoons white wine

4 tablespoons butter

about ½ cup finely grated Gruyère

a good pinch of black pepper

For poaching

sufficient court bouillon for nonoily fish (p. 28) to cover the fish

For the garnish

2 tablespoons finely grated Parmesan

1 tablespoon finely chopped parsley

The sauce should be made just before poaching begins and kept hot. Loosen the velouté with the white wine. Fold in the butter and cook gently, stirring briskly for 5 minutes. Off the heat, stir in the Gruyère and the pepper. Keep stirring until the cheese has dissolved and combined with the sauce.

Poach the fillets of sole in the court bouillon for 4 minutes. Drain and place them in a heated shallow ovenproof dish. Cover with the hot Mornay sauce, and sprinkle with the Parmesan. Put on the upper shelf of a hot, 450°F oven for 5 minutes to brown. Garnish with the parsley.

VARIATION

Mornay sauce is adaptable for use with all the finest firm fish, as well as softer and cheaper varieties.

Cook and dress in the same way fillets of flounder, haddock, or thin steaks of cod, hake, pollock, ling, though all these softer fish should initially be poached for only 2½ minutes before being drained, masked with sauce, and put in the oven to brown.

COD WITH EGG AND PARSLEY SAUCE

Cod is a marvelous but delicate fish that is easily overcooked. This is a simple and very British dish.

SERVES 4

4 cod steaks of about 6 ounces each

For poaching

court bouillon for nonoily fish (p. 28) to cover

For the sauce

2 tablespoons finely chopped parsley

1 teaspoon finely chopped chives

2½ cups fish velouté sauce (p. 20)

salt and black pepper to taste

3 eggs, hard-boiled and coarsely chopped

For the garnish

watercress

lemon quarters

Poach the steaks in the court bouillon for 3 minutes. Probe and, if cooked, drain and remove to a deep serving dish and keep hot. Now blend the parsley and chives with the velouté. Season with salt and pepper. Finally, add the chopped eggs. Pour the sauce over the steaks in the deep dish. Garnish with the watercress and lemon quarters.

Halibut with Cream and Butter Sauce

The halibut is a meaty, firm fish which, though famous for its vitamin-rich liver oil, is in the nonoily class. Steaks from the upper and middle part of the fish are juiciest; at the tail end they tend to dryness.

SERVES 5–6

2 pounds halibut steaks	1 sprig of thyme
For the sauce	6 ounces unsalted butter
scant ⅔ cup water	1¼ cups heavy cream
1 shallot, finely chopped	**For poaching**
1 teaspoon ground allspice	court bouillon for nonoily fish (p. 28) to cover
1 teaspoon ground black pepper	**For the garnish**
a good pinch of salt	sprigs of parsley
1 small bay leaf	lemon quarters

Put the first seven sauce ingredients into a pan. Reduce the liquid, by boiling, to a tablespoon of concentrated flavor. Melt the butter in a pan and pour in the concentrate, filtered through a sieve. Beat the liquid and butter together well. Place over very low heat, and as the butter gets hot, slowly pour in the cream, beating all the while. Keep hot in a bain-marie (p. 14), beating from time to time, as you poach the fish.

Poach the steaks in the court bouillon for 6 minutes. Then probe at the central bone. When ready, remove the steaks to a hot serving dish and spoon a little of the sauce over each one. Garnish with parsley and lemon quarters. Serve the rest of the sauce separately.

This sauce is another quick, simple one for general use. It is variable with a change of herbs and spices and especially good with fillets of the cod family.

Salmon with Béarnaise Sauce

If, for a special occasion, a salmon or salmon trout comes your way, a fish kettle will be needed: a kettle which will nicely accommodate a fish of about 4 pounds. This should feed sufficient people to make the event memorable and leave some scraps for a new dish next day.

SERVES 10–12

1 salmon weighing 4 pounds	2 pinches of salt
For the sauce	**For poaching**
2 shallots, finely chopped	4–5 quarts court bouillon for oil-rich fish (p. 28), made with vinegar in the proportion of scant ⅔ cup to every 5 cups court bouillon
scant 2 cups wine vinegar, preferably tarragon	
3 egg yolks	
½ pound butter, cut in 1-inch pieces	**For the garnish**
2 tablespoons finely chopped fresh tarragon	sprigs of parsley
1 teaspoon freshly and finely ground black pepper	1 cucumber, peeled and finely sliced
	2 lemons, finely sliced

Boil the shallots in the vinegar until they are reduced to a puree and only 4–5 tablespoons of the liquid are left. Strain the liquid into a saucepan, and allow to cool. Then, over very low heat, beat the egg yolks in well. Now add the butter, piece by piece, whisking vigorously throughout the process. Fold in the tarragon, pepper, and salt. Keep the sauce warm in its pan, whisking from time to time, at the side of the stove or in a bain-marie (p. 14) until the salmon is poached.

Put the fish on the lifting tray of the fish kettle,

and lower it into the cool court bouillon. Bring slowly to the simmering point and poach gently for 16 minutes, when it should be cooked. Test with a sharp knife in the thickest part. Slowly lift the fish out of the kettle and onto its tray, allowing it to drain well. Transfer to a hot serving dish. Now carefully remove the skin from the side displayed and adorn with sprigs of parsley around the sides and very thin rounds of cucumber and lemon to form a pattern on the top. Serve the sauce separately.

The béarnaise is another great classic sauce, based on the technique of the hollandaise, which goes well with all kinds of fish. Made with olive oil instead of butter it is especially useful with cold fish. The name *béarnaise* applies specifically to the sauce made with tarragon. However, other herbs and spices may be substituted, e.g., capers, horseradish, chervil, celery, or garlic, to provide a wide range of fine sauces.

MONKFISH WITH A RICH TOMATO SAUCE

Poor monkfish, branded one of nature's ugliest creatures, with its enormous mouth and a fishing rod sprouting from its brow, to tempt unwary small fry to their doom. Seldom is the ungainly head displayed on the fishmonger's slab, but I have grown familiar with it, living here in Cyprus. It would make a splendid villain in a children's book of submarine fantasies. However, for our purposes, what is most important about the monkfish is that its flavor has some affinity with that of the lobster and the scallop.

SERVES 6

2 pounds monkfish, cut into 2-inch pieces	4 tablespoons butter
For poaching	1 tablespoon olive oil
sufficient court bouillon for nonoily fish (p. 28) to cover the fish	1 tablespoon finely chopped parsley
For the sauce	1 teaspoon finely chopped basil
2 pounds fresh tomatoes, peeled	1 teaspoon ground black pepper
scant ⅔ cup red wine	1 teaspoon creamed horseradish
juice of 1 lemon	1 teaspoon grated gingerroot
2 cloves garlic, pounded	
3 small anchovy fillets, pounded	

Pack the fish pieces into the smallest pan that will enable them to lie comfortably on the bottom. Cover with the court bouillon. Bring to the simmering point and cook for 8 minutes. Probe with a sharp knife to see if they are cooked. Now chop and pound the tomatoes; put them in a pan with the wine and lemon juice. Cook briskly, stirring, until reduced to a thick puree. In a separate pan, over low heat, sauté half the garlic with the pounded anchovy in the butter and the oil. Before the garlic changes color, add the tomato puree and the parsley. Cook together until the mixture becomes very stiff. Remove from the heat and work into the mixture the basil and the remaining garlic, pounded with the black pepper, horseradish, and ginger. Now loosen the mixture with about 2 cups of the stock in which the fish was poached. Transfer the fish to a heated serving dish. Pour over the sauce and serve.

4
BAKING

Baking implies cooking in a more or less hot oven with little or no liquid. Most fish would dry out if exposed to the heat of the oven without some means of moistening them, so it is customary to provide a source, however meager, of liquid, butter, or oil, with herbs and aromatics, with which the fish can be basted. This also contributes savor to the hot air circulating around it as it cooks.

Small oil-rich fish such as herring and mackerel need less basting than nonoily fish because they give off some moisture from their skins.

Whole baked fish look attractive and can be served from the dish in which they are cooked.

BAKED HERRINGS WITH MUSTARD BUTTER

The herring, weight for weight, is as nutritious as meat. It would be a crime if overfishing were to eliminate it from the nation's diet. It is oil-rich and does not require a rich sauce. A sharp relish or mustard butter will point up its unique flavor. Broiling or baking them whole retains this flavor to a great degree. In cooking them open a good deal of flavor is lost, as is the joy of slitting them down the back on one's plate and inhaling the first savory vapors.

SERVES 4

four 8-ounce herrings	4 tablespoons mustard
For baking	butter, softened (p. 18)
2 teaspoons unsalted butter	1 lemon

Rub the unsalted butter around the bottom and sides of a shallow baking dish. Score the herrings diagonally on one side, deeply but not down to the bone, and

lay them, cut side up, in the baking dish. Rub the fish with the softened mustard butter, making sure that the gashes are filled. Put them in a 400°F oven for 7 minutes. Remove from the oven, turn the fish over carefully, and again score them diagonally, taking care to avoid lining up with the cuts on the other side. Smear the fish with the mustard butter in the cuts, as before. Put them back in the oven for 5 minutes more. Again remove from the oven, baste the exposed surfaces of the fish, and raise the oven to 450°. Wait 1 minute for the temperature to rise. Put the fish back, this time on the topmost shelf of the oven, for 2 minutes. Serve with quarters of lemon, salt, and pepper.

To accompany the fish, make a plateful of watercress or mustard-and-cress sandwiches, using thin brown bread and butter.

SEA BREAM WITH PIMIENTO SAUCE

The bream family comes in all sizes and colors, from the 4-inch pickerel to the majestic dentex. Between these are the sea breams familiar to the British market. Oval in shape, they appear to suffer from slight spinal curvature due to their ponderous heads. They are splendid food, with easily avoided bones; good oval steaks can be got from the larger ones.

SERVES 5–6

1 sea bream weighing about 2 pounds	For baking
For the sauce	2 tablespoons olive oil
5 small red peppers	juice of 1 lemon
about 2 cups béchamel sauce (p. 19)	salt and ground black pepper
2 good pinches of ground allspice	1 large Spanish onion, very finely sliced and separated into rings

Blanch the peppers in boiling water for 1 minute. When cool, remove stalk, pith, and seeds. Chop the peppers finely and blend into a puree with a few tablespoons of béchamel and then return this to the rest. Add the allspice. The sauce is now ready and should be kept hot, but not allowed to boil.

Brush the fish, inside and out, with a mixture of oil and lemon, salt and pepper. Likewise brush the inside of a wide shallow baking dish. Lay half the onion rings in the dish. Place the fish on them, and use the remaining onion rings to cover the top of the fish. Put the dish into a 350°F oven for 25 minutes. Remove from the oven. Slide the onion rings off the top and again brush the fish with the basting mixture. Raise the oven to 425°F and cook the fish for another 7–8 minutes.

I suggest ratatouille (p. 39) as an accompaniment.

BAKED RED MULLET WITH A RATATOUILLE

These delicious fish, which are not related to the gray mullet, are now hardly to be found larger than 4 inches long in the Mediterranean, but they are sometimes found in larger sizes in fish markets. They are rightly considered to be one of the finest flavored of all the round fish. (The addition of one small red mullet to a fish stock imparts a very special, gamey flavor to the velouté sauces and soups for which the stock is used.)

SERVES 4

12 small 3-ounce red mullet or 8 of a larger size: say, 6 ounces

For the ratatouille

½ cup olive oil

2 large onions, finely sliced

3 cloves garlic, crushed

4 small eggplant, thickly chopped

1 large green pepper, deseeded and coarsely chopped

1 large red pepper, deseeded and coarsely chopped

4 peeled tomatoes

salt and pepper to taste

For baking

2 shallots, finely chopped

1 small carrot, grated

6 tablespoons butter

1 tablespoon finely chopped parsley

1 tablespoon finely chopped fennel leaves

a scattering of ground black pepper

a pinch of salt

In the olive oil, cook the onions and the garlic until both are soft, but do not let them take color. Add the eggplant and the green and red peppers. Cook these together for 10 minutes. Add the tomatoes and the salt and pepper. Cover the pan and allow to stew very gently over a very low heat for 1 hour.

In a shallow fireproof dish, on top of the stove, simmer the shallots and the carrot in the butter till tender. Sprinkle with the parsley and fennel, pepper and salt, and stir around for 30 seconds. Lay the fish down on this buttery bed and move them around for a few moments. Then turn them over so that both sides of all the fish are covered with butter. Now, if the fish are small ones, put the dish into a hot 450°F oven. After 3 minutes they should be turned and baked for 3 minutes more. If your fish are the larger ones, the oven should be set at 400° and the mullets baked for 5 minutes before turning and baking for another 5 minutes.

Serve the mullets in the baking dish, spooning the buttery mixture over the fish before you do so. Lemon juice is the only sauce required. Pass the ratatouille separately.

BAKED CARP PROVENÇAL

This is a south of France treatment for freshwater fish which can, however, also be applied to any sizable sea fish that comes your way. It is also a *minceur* dish, as it includes no butter, oil, milk, or flour.

SERVES 6–8

one 2-pound carp	2 tablespoons finely
the white of 4 leeks, finely sliced	chopped celeriac
1 carrot, grated	2 tablespoons finely chopped fennel root
1 large onion, finely sliced	1 sprig of rosemary
2 sweet peppers, cleaned, deseeded, and chopped	3 cloves garlic, chopped and pounded
1 eggplant finely sliced	1¼ cups red wine
4 tomatoes, peeled and coarsely chopped	1 teaspoon salt
	1 teaspoon black pepper

In a baking dish that will comfortably accommodate the fish, lay down a bed of all the vegetables and herbs listed above. Moisten it with half the wine and season with salt and pepper. Lay the fish on this savory bed and put it into the middle of a preheated 350°F oven. Let it cook for 45 minutes, then test with a sharp-pointed knife, near the spine. Remove the fish to a large serving dish. Open it down the back and remove the main bone. Cover and keep hot. Now, on the top of the stove, add the rest of the wine to the medley of herbs and vegetables. Cook at a brisk pace as you stir vigorously for 3 or 4 minutes. Pour all, piping hot, over the open fish in the serving dish. Serve with green lentils and a potato or chestnut puree.

RED SNAPPER BAKED WITH VEGETABLES

Always popular in America, this delicious fish is now an international favorite. Both the large and small snappers are particularly suitable for baking and braising.

SERVES 4

4 red snappers, about 7 ounces each	¾ cup olive oil
For baking	juice of 1 lemon
2 good pinches of ground allspice	a choice of vegetables from the following: small potatoes, whole small onions, baby carrots or large ones sliced, turnips, sweet peppers, zucchini, cauliflower florets
2 good pinches of ground ginger	
2 good pinches of ground cumin	

Blend the spices with the olive oil and lemon juice. Boil your selection of, say, four vegetables, separately and gently for 10 minutes each. Drain and set aside to cool a little. Then brush the vegetables with the spiced oil mixture. Place them in a circle around the baking dish.

Brush the snappers, inside and out, with the same mixture as that used on the vegetables and place them in the center of the baking dish. Set to cook in a 400°F oven for 20 minutes. Test with a sharp-pointed knife at the backbone, to confirm. By this time the vegetables should be completely cooked and pleasantly browned at the edges.

Serve in the baking dish.

FRESH TUNA SWEET AND SOUR

The tuna is an oil-rich fish, very firm in texture, and goes further than most other fish; it needs no heavy, rich sauce to accompany it. It is at its best as here, where a marinade, with a small addition, becomes the sauce.

SERVES 6

2 pounds tuna,
in small fillets or
divided steaks

For the marinade

1 tablespoon Spanish or
other onion juice

1 teaspoon soy sauce

1 teaspoon honey or
sugar

1 tablespoon wine vinegar

juice of 1 lemon

2 bay leaves, bruised

3 tablespoons olive oil

1 teaspoon finely ground
black pepper

For the sauce

1 tablespoon tomato paste

scant ⅔ cup dry red wine

Blend together the marinade ingredients and lay the fish in the marinade in a dish that just fits. Turn the fillets or steaks over from time to time, for a period of 30 minutes. Then remove them from the marinade and put them in a baking dish in which they fit in a single layer.

Bake in a preheated 400°F oven. Baste with the marinade if necessary. They will take 12–15 minutes, depending on the thickness of the fish, turning them once at half time. Remove the fillets or steaks to a covered serving dish to keep hot.

Now put the marinade into a saucepan and add to it the tomato paste and the dry red wine. Cook briskly for 4 minutes. Remove the bay leaves, spoon the mixture over the tuna fish, and serve.

VARIATION

Salmon fillets and steaks also respond well to this sweet-and-sour treatment.

COOKING AU GRATIN

The gratin produces a lovely upper crust when done right. Simple gratins are easily made. It is a useful method of serving fillets, steaks, or other cuts of fish, which are poached to a point just before they are fully cooked, and then masked with a sauce that will brown quickly under high heat. Thickish butter sauces sprinkled with bread crumbs are good for this purpose, but the obvious sauce to use here is the Mornay (p. 33). Even when the fish masked by the sauce is already fully cooked, the speed at which the sauce acquires its lovely crust under a hot broiler should enable the dish to be a success. This is another method for regular use in dressing fish.

What is called a "full gratin" is not quite so simple. In this, uncooked fish is combined in a dish with a sauce which must itself cook and thicken with the fish and its juices, at the same time acquiring that splendid upper crust; and all this is to be done in the oven.

PAUPIETTES OF SOLE FLORENTINE AU GRATIN

Stuffed fillets of Dover sole: this is one of the best ways of serving this fine-flavored and firm-textured fish. Here, sandwiched between two layers of savory spinach, it makes, with the addition of grated cheese and bread crumbs, a splendid gratin.

SERVES 6

six 4-ounce fillets of Dover sole, with the white skin left on

For the stuffing

2 teaspoons olive oil

5 small mushrooms, chopped

2 shallots, finely chopped

1 anchovy fillet, pounded

1 tablespoon fine white bread crumbs

1 tablespoon tomato paste

1 tablespoon finely chopped basil

2 teaspoons Madeira

5 single drops of Tabasco or 1 pinch of cayenne pepper

juice of 1 lemon

For the 2 sides of the "sandwich"

1 pound cooked and drained spinach

1 tablespoon chopped parsley

1 pinch of ground nutmeg

1 pinch of ground allspice

½ teaspoon salt

½ teaspoon black pepper

scant ⅔ cup heavy cream, thoroughly beaten with 1 whole egg

For the gratin topping

1 cup fine bread crumbs

4 tablespoons butter, softened

¼ cup finely grated Parmesan

2 tablespoons finely grated Gruyère

1 teaspoon prepared English mustard

First make the stuffing. Cook the mushrooms and shallots in the oil until they begin to take color. Add this mixture (a simple *duxelles*) to all the other ingredients, and blend in a food processor.

Now make the "sandwich" mixture by adding all the other listed ingredients to the spinach and blending well.

Lay the fillets, skin side down, on a board, and spread the stuffing evenly over them. Roll them up, and either tie them with thin string or secure them by pinning with a toothpick. Line the bottom of a baking dish with half the spinach mixture. Lay the fillets in a row on this bed. Cover with the remaining spinach, creating a nice fit. Cover and put the dish into the middle of a preheated 350°F oven and cook for 25 minutes. At the end of that time remove the dish from the oven, take off the lid, and with a spatula spread the gratin mixture evenly over the top. Return to the oven, uncovered this time, and raise the temperature to 400° for 12 minutes more.

Serve a beurre blanc (butter and wine sauce) separately (see below).

Note: this recipe for Dover sole starts as an almost dry braise, and only becomes a gratin in its final uncovered stage, where it takes on a fine color.

BEURRE BLANC

2 shallots, finely chopped

⅓ cup white wine

⅓ cup white wine vinegar

½ pound unsalted butter

good pinches of salt and finely ground black pepper

In a saucepan, cook the shallots in the wine and vinegar until reduced to 2 tablespoonsful. Strain through a sieve into another pan, and over low heat beat in the butter, in small pieces, one by one, until it is all absorbed and the sauce looks like well-whipped cream. Taste, and season with salt and pepper if necessary. This sauce is one of the most delicate in flavor and is best used with all good nonoily fish.

FILLETS OF MONKFISH AU GRATIN

SERVES 4

four 6-ounce ½ inch-thick cuts of monkfish, dusted with 2 tablespoons flour and then shaken

For the sauce

1 tablespoon olive oil

¼ pound mushrooms, finely chopped

¼ pound onion, finely chopped

3 tablespoons flour

2½ cups fish stock (p. 30)

about 6 tablespoons tomato paste

2 tablespoons red wine

1 tablespoon finely chopped fennel leaves

1 tablespoon finely chopped parsley

1 tablespoon finely chopped basil

pinch of pepper and salt

pinch of ground cumin

1 cup fresh bread crumbs

Lay the fillets dusted with flour in a shallow baking dish that will comfortably hold them and 2½ cups of the sauce. Set aside. Into a small saucepan, put the oil. Add the mushrooms and onions, and cook over low heat until they begin to take color. Remove the pan from the heat and stir in the flour. Return to the heat and moisten the mixture with half the fish stock. Stir vigorously, then allow to cook for 1 minute. Now— off the heat again—put in the tomato paste and again loosen the mixture with the rest of the fish stock and the wine. Add the fennel, parsley, basil, pepper, salt, and cumin. Mix all together well and pour over the floured fish in the dish. Put the dish into a 375°F oven for 20 minutes. Remove and sprinkle with the bread crumbs. Now raise the oven heat to 425°, allowing 5 minutes for it to become stabilized at the higher setting. Return the dish to the oven for 10 minutes.

5

BRAISING

Broiling, poaching, and baking are quite clear-cut techniques of fish cookery. Braising, a process invented for the slow cooking of the tougher cuts of meat, would appear to have no proper place in fish cookery, where toughness hardly exists. Any whole fine, firm fish of impressive size, however, repays the trouble of braising it, and I have chosen some of the handsomest fish for these recipes.

The fish is cooked with vegetables and herbs and a small quantity of liquid, which is reduced or thickened at the end of cooking to make a sauce. Braising allows the flavor of the fish and the vegetables and aromatics to blend thoroughly.

COOKING "KLEFTIKO" OR EN PAPILLOTE
The "kleftiko" or "thieves' kitchen" method of cooking originated in ancient times when outlaws and poachers would cook their wrapped meats in sealed earth-covered ovens so that no smoke or scent should betray their whereabouts. With the advent of high-quality foil, this form of cooking has made a strong bid to supersede both poaching and braising.

Clearly it is a sensible and clean way of cooking large fish without having to make stock separately. With smaller fish, too, and small cuts of firm fish, these silver parcels impart a spirit of gift giving to the occasion. The way each person unwraps the fish present and greets the first scents is an entertainment in itself.

I have found problems in establishing cooking times for these fish parcels, for once they generate internal steam, cooking can be faster than in the poaching process and, what is more, can go on for a considerable time after they have been removed from the oven.

Soft fish, however excellent, are not recommended for this form of cooking. I shall only give, therefore, a tentative recipe for dealing with a 6-ounce steak of any firm fish en papillote.

For inclusion in the parcel with the fish: a choice of either 2 tablespoons of any of the relishes for which a pattern is given on p. 16, or 4 tablespoons of any of the savory butters for which a similar pattern is given on p. 18.

Wrap the steak and its accompaniments in a parcel as airtight as you can create. Place in a preheated 350°F oven for 10 minutes. Inspect for any sign of cooking within. If this is observed, leave the parcel for another 2 minutes; if none, leave longer. Then remove it and transfer the contents to a heated plate.

SALMON TROUT EN PAPILLOTTE

We follow the normal procedure and are left, when the fish is cooked, with a residue in the foil of juices of the fish itself and whatever else we have put into the parcel.

Using this residue, *soi-même* sauces (p. 19) can be quickly made while the fish is kept covered and warm in the bottom of an oven set at 275°F or less. This recipe shows the sort of thing that can be done.

SERVES 6

one 2-pound salmon trout	**For the sauce**
6 scrupulously clean unopened mussels	the strained residues from the foil in which the fish has been cooked
1 tablespoon finely chopped celery heart	
1 bay leaf	2 egg yolks, well beaten with scant 1 cup heavy cream
1 tablespoon white wine vinegar	4 tablespoons butter, softened
1 tablespoon medium-dry white wine	**For the garnish**
juice of ½ lemon	8 black olives, pitted
pinch of ground allspice	1 small bunch of watercress
½ teaspoon salt	

Make up a foil parcel containing the whole salmon trout, the mussels, and all the other ingredients. Close it tightly to ensure that nothing leaks out. Place the parcel on a baking tray in the middle of a preheated 350°F oven for 35 minutes. Remove from the oven. Allow the parcel to "settle down" for a minute. Then open it.

Lift out the trout and put it into a covered serving dish to keep warm at the bottom of a low oven. Set the mussels aside.

In making the sauce, speed is now of the essence. Strain the residues in the foil into a saucepan and boil quickly to reduce by a third. Remove from the heat and allow to drop well below the boiling point. (An ice cube comes in handy here.) Now beat in the egg-and-cream mixture over very low heat or in a bain-marie. Continue to beat as you fold in the butter. Beat until the sauce starts to thicken. Remove from the heat and keep hot.

Remove the trout from the oven. Open it down the back and extract the main bone. Garnish the fish with a few tablespoons of the sauce and decorate with the olives, mussels, and sprigs of watercress. Serve the rest of the sauce separately.

Note: the very special cachet given by the mussels, which open inside the foil package to disgorge their marvelous juices, justifies that modest bivalve's claim to be "the truffle of the sea."

GRAY MULLET BRAISED WITH SORREL AND LETTUCE

If you can't get sorrel, you can substitute spinach, or make the dish just with lettuce, but the flavor will not be as good.

SERVES 4

1 gray mullet weighing about 2 pounds	scant ⅔ cup dry vermouth
1 Romaine lettuce	6 tablespoons heavy cream
½ pound sorrel	
4 tablespoons butter	salt and pepper
2 shallots, finely chopped	

Wash the lettuce, drain well, and shred it finely. Wash and drain the sorrel and remove the stalks. Heat the butter in an ovenproof dish that will hold the fish comfortably and cook the shallots gently for 5 minutes.

Add the shredded lettuce and the sorrel and cook, stirring from time to time, until the lettuce has wilted.

Spread out the vegetables to make a bed for the fish and season with salt and pepper. Put the fish into the dish and pour over the vermouth. Cover with a lid or a well-fitting piece of foil and transfer to a preheated 375°F oven for 30 minutes.

Remove from the oven, put the mullet on a warmed serving dish, and surround with the greens. Keep warm.

Strain the cooking liquid into a pan and boil for a few minutes to reduce somewhat. Lower the heat, stir in the cream, and pour the sauce over the fish. Serve at once.

SWORDFISH BRAISED IN TOMATO SAUCE

SERVES 4

4 swordfish steaks, about 1 inch thick	1½ pounds tomatoes, peeled, seeded, and chopped
3 tablespoons olive oil	salt and pepper
3 cloves garlic, finely chopped	bouquet garni
1 large onion, finely chopped	juice of ½ lemon

Heat the oil in a large pan, add the garlic and onion and cook for a few minutes, then put in the tomatoes. Stew gently for 15 minutes. Put in the swordfish steaks, season all with salt and pepper, and tuck in the bouquet garni. Add a little water, if necessary, so that the fish is barely covered.

Cover the pan tightly and braise in a preheated 350°F oven for 25 minutes, or until the fish is cooked. Transfer the fish to a serving dish and keep warm. If the sauce looks a little thin, boil for a few minutes to reduce it. Discard the bouquet garni. Stir in the lemon juice, pour the sauce over the fish and serve.

Braised Sea Bass in a Velouté Sauce

This recipe enables us to produce in one pot the court bouillon for the fish to cook in, the fish stock with which the velouté sauce is made, and the garnish for the fish. It also demonstrates that valuable technique, the blending together of flour and butter (beurre manié) for binding and thickening a strong fish stock and producing, as it were in reverse, a splendid fish velouté sauce.

SERVES 8–10

1 sea bass, approximately 4–5 pounds

For the court bouillon

3 quarts water

1¼ cups red or white dry wine

4 whites of leek, coarsely chopped

4 medium-size carrots, cut into long strips

4 or 5 medium-size onions, halved

For the sauce

3¾ cups liquid from the fish kettle

6 tablespoons butter, softened

⅔ cup flour

4 celery hearts, cut into lengthwise strips

2 green peppers, deseeded and cut into strips

2 red peppers, deseeded and cut into strips

2 cloves garlic, crushed

1 teaspoon ground black pepper

1 teaspoon salt

1 teaspoon ground allspice

3 bouquets garnis

For the garnish

lemon quarters

Put all the ingredients for the court bouillon into a small fish kettle and cook together for 20 minutes. There should be enough liquid remaining to cover the vegetables. Remove from the heat and allow to cool and the ingredients to infuse. Preheat the oven to 325°F. Now move the vegetables and herbs to the sides of the tray of the fish kettle, making room for the fish in the middle. The liquid should come up to a third of the depth of the fish. Place over a low heat, cover, and slowly bring to the simmering point. Unless the fish is very cold, this should not take long. As soon as the simmering begins, heap the vegetables around the fish, but not so as to cover it entirely. Cover the kettle tightly and put it in the preheated oven. After 4 minutes, check to see that it is simmering gently. Replace the lid closely and cook for 25 minutes. Now remove the kettle from the oven and slowly lift out the tray of fish and vegetables, so that the liquid drains back into the kettle. Reserve the liquid. Slide the fish onto a wide, heated serving dish, arranging the strips of vegetables around it and removing the bouquets garnis. Cover to keep hot.

To make the sauce: ladle 3¾ cups of the braising liquid into a saucepan and cook over low heat. Blend the butter and flour together, and when the liquid comes to the boil, drop the flour and butter mixture, little by little, into it until it begins to thicken. Continue the process until you have a good thick velouté sauce.

Keep the sauce hot while, with a sharp knife, you cut the fish open down the back. Open it out wide on the dish and extract the main bone. Spoon the sliced vegetables over the top of the very white flesh and take to the table. Serve the sauce separately. Garnish the dish with quarters of lemon.

A hazard of this style of cooking is the uncertainty of braising time in the oven, for if the simmering stops, then the fish probably will not be cooked in the time stated. One cannot keep taking the lid off to inspect every 2 or 3 minutes, but testing after the first 4 minutes is advised.

BRAISED DOGFISH TANANARIVE

Good firm, nonoily fish of the smaller shark family have, over recent years, become deservedly popular. Fillets of dogfish, tope, huss and catfish have always been fine eating when, fried in deep fat at the fried-fish shop, they were all lumped together under the one, unnecessarily deceptive, name of "rock salmon." These firm fish, full of the flavor of the sea, are particularly good when treated as in the preceding recipe: braised in a good wine stock and accompanied by a sauce made from the juice of the fish as it cooks. The following recipe can be applied to all four of the fish named above, and indeed to any firm nonoily fish.

SERVES 4–6

2 pounds thickly cut pieces of dogfish	1 teaspoon salt
5 cups court bouillon	1 teaspoon ground black pepper
For the court bouillon	**For the sauce**
5 cups water	6 tablespoons beurre manié (p. 15)
scant ⅔ cup white wine	12 finely ground green peppercorns
1 carrot, grated	
2 onions, chopped	
1 celery heart, chopped	1 tablespoon finely chopped parsley
1 clove garlic, crushed	
3 sprigs of parsley	

For dealing with these cuts of firm fish we do not need a large vessel, such as a fish kettle, but rather the smallest lidded pan that will accept them, loosely packed together, leaving room for as much court bouillon as will barely cover them and yet supply enough liquid for a fine, strongly flavored sauce when the braising is done. You must use your judgment here.

Boil all the ingredients for the court bouillon for 25 minutes. Allow to stand, uncovered, and get cool.

Put the pieces of fish into the braising pan, loosely packed together. When the stock is cool, strain it onto the fish and shake the pan so that the liquid settles down into the crevices. The liquid should be barely enough to cover the top surfaces of the fish. Retain any surplus stock for later use in a sauce or a soup. Preheat the oven to 325°F. On top of the cooker, bring the stock to the simmering point. Cover and transfer to the preheated oven. After 2 minutes, check to see that the stock is still simmering. Put the cover back and allow to cook for 8 minutes. Then transfer the pan to the top of the stove and allow to stand, covered, for 5 minutes. Remove the pieces of fish to a hot, deep serving dish and keep warm.

There should now be at least 2½ cups of rich fish stock in the pan. Bring this to a boil and drop in the beurre manié, in pieces, stirring vigorously. When the liquid begins to thicken, reduce the heat and add, first, the finely ground green peppercorns and, one minute later, the finely chopped parsley. Stir well. Pour the hot sauce over the fish in the deep serving dish. Serve with thoroughly drained spinach and well-buttered mashed potatoes.

49

6
FRYING

The essentials to the method are good, clean oil and a sound, fresh batter. I prefer olive oil, but any good peanut or sunflower oil would be suitable for frying.

DEEP-FRYING

I blame the addiction of the public to deep-frying in batter for much of the present almost hostile attitude toward fish in general, and toward the cooking of it at home in particular. If cooking oil is used over and over again and small stale fragments of fish or batter remain in it, it produces a nauseating odor which has absolutely no connection with fresh fish or good oil. That said, those cooks prepared to take the trouble should not be denied a very valuable and flavor-retaining method of cooking small whole fish, fillets, cuts, and steaks of every kind.

Fish for deep frying: especially suited to deep-frying in batter are fillets of cod, fresh haddock, lemon sole, flounder and whiting.

To deep-fry whitebait, those delicious nurslings of many different types of fish, no batter is required. They should simply be tumbled about in a bag with a small quantity of flour. Removed from the bag, they should be shaken out to dislodge extra flour and then put into the hot frying basket.

BASIC BATTER

MAKES ENOUGH TO COVER
4 SERVINGS OF FISH

about ⅓ cup flour	*a pinch of salt*
1 whole egg	*scant ⅔ cup milk*

Put the flour into a bowl. Make a hollow in the middle and put in the egg. With a wooden spoon, stir around and around so that the egg gradually mixes with the flour and both are well blended together and smooth. Then add the salt; pour in the milk gradually, blending it in. Leave the batter to stand for 30 minutes or so before using. When the fish, coated in batter, goes into the basket of the deep-frying pan, the temperature of the oil should be between 312° and 325°F. Test with a small piece of bread, which should quickly turn a pale brown, but get no darker. Most fish deep-fried in batter will rise to the surface when cooked. Scoop them out with a perforated cooking spatula and drain on paper towels. Do not crowd the pan with too many pieces of fish.

SHALLOW FRYING

A much smaller quantity of oil is needed in shallow frying; in an ordinary frying pan it should only come halfway up the thickness of the fish being cooked. Fillets of all the fish mentioned above under Deep-Frying, except whitebait, are better and more conveniently cooked this way, first on one side, then on the other. The fillets should be dipped into seasoned beaten egg, then rolled in bread crumbs, before they are put into the pan of hot oil.

A NOTE ON SAUCES FOR FRIED FISH

The relish (p. 16) is an ingrained habit and not a bad one: a glance back will refresh your memory of the variety of these and the speed with which they can be put together. However, I favor the following classic sauces, which, made before frying begins, immediately turn our fried-fish dinner into a gourmet feast: gribiche (p. 31), tartare (p. 32), béarnaise (p. 34), hollandaise (p. 20).

FRYING *À LA MEUNIÈRE*

Cooking *à la meunière* is not only by far the best method of frying but also one of the best ways of all of cooking fish. Briefly, it is the quick, light frying of fillets or whole flat fish, dusted with flour, in really hot butter. When the fish is cooked on both sides, it is removed from the pan, to which more butter is added and then swirled around until foaming. The juice of half a lemon is then introduced, together with a tablespoon of finely chopped parsley. This piping-hot mixture is poured over the fish, which has been kept hot in a heated serving dish. The only sauce needed is the butter.

FLOUNDER *À LA MEUNIÈRE*

SERVES 4

four 6-ounce fillets of flounder	2 pinches of salt
scant ¼ cup flour	juice of 1 lemon
¼ pound unsalted butter	2 tablespoons finely chopped parsley
2 pinches of ground black pepper	1 lemon, quartered

Dust the fillets of flounder with flour. Shake well to remove any extra. Put half the butter in the pan and, when hot, put the fillets in to cook. After 3 minutes, turn them over, and cook for 3 minutes more. Remove them to a heated serving dish. Now put the rest of the butter into the pan with the seasonings. Stir all around until the hot butter begins to foam. Pour in the lemon juice, down the side of the pan, and add the parsley. Stir all around and pour, piping hot, over the fillets in the serving dish. Serve with quarters of lemon.

Note: for all cooking *à la meunière*, unsalted or clarified butter is essential; although it should become nut-brown when very hot, it should not be allowed to burn. The addition of a teaspoon of oil at the earliest stage of the frying helps to avoid subsequent burning and does not invalidate the recipe.

VARIATION

Use lemon sole instead of flounder.

FRITTO MISTO

For this simple "fry-up," it is best to choose from either fillets of all firm fish, such as sole, turbot, brill, and monkfish, or all soft fish, such as flounder, cod, hake, lemon sole, and haddock, so that all the fish will be cooked at roughly the same rate. In this recipe, firm fish is used.

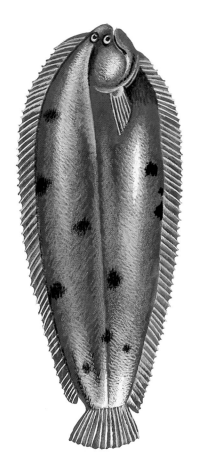

SERVES 4–6

6 ounces fillet of sole	1 tablespoon finely
6 ounces fillet of brill	chopped parsley
6 ounces fillet of monkfish	**For the sauce**
4 scallops	3 tablespoons olive
4 large cooked shrimp	or nut oil
sufficient oil to cover the frying pan to the depth of ¼ inch	1 clove garlic, crushed
	2 shallots, finely chopped
¾ cup batter (p. 50)	1 pound tomatoes, peeled and finely chopped
¼ pound small mushrooms, quartered by cutting down through the stalks twice	salt and pepper
	For the garnish
	lemon segments

Make the sauce first. In the pan, sauté the garlic and shallots in the oil until they are soft but have not changed color. Add the tomatoes, salt, and pepper and cook vigorously until it becomes a thickish puree. Set aside and keep hot.

Cut the fillets of fish into 1-ounce pieces. Bisect the scallops horizontally through the white flesh. Separate the coral "cock's combs." Peel and bisect the shrimp, head to tail. Set the scallop and shrimp pieces aside until the fillets have been cooked. Roll the pieces of fish in the batter and let them stand for 10 minutes. Meanwhile, heat the oil in the pan until it is almost smoking. Put in the fish and cook until nicely browned on both sides. Remove them, using a perforated cooking spatula, to a warm serving dish. Cover and keep warm in the bottom of a low oven. Now, having removed any particles of singed batter from the oil remaining in the pan, toss in the pieces of mushroom and shellfish and move them around for 3 minutes. Take the pan from the heat and scatter the parsley over all. Retrieve the fried fish pieces from the oven and pour the contents of the pan over them. Make a space in the middle of the dish into which the thick tomato sauce can now be poured. Adorn the rim of the dish with segments of lemon.

7

SHELLFISH & CEPHALOPODS

My arbitrary separation, up to now, of the round and flat fish from their marine cousins and collaterals, the shellfish—under which term I include all shellfish from the crustacean-like lobster to the winkle we eat with a pin—requires some explanation.

Under self-imposed sumptuary laws and in a sincere missionary spirit, I have so far withheld from the sauce recipes—which usually give their names to the dishes with which they are served—that enrichment first with egg yolks, cream, and butter, then with garnishes of shellfish and other expensive delicacies, which would entitle them to awesome menu names. Some examples are the following, which demand for garnish, after the egg yolk, cream, and butter enrichment: *Nantua*, poached oysters and slices of truffles; *Normande*, poached oysters and mussels, prawns, shrimps, gudgeons, crayfish, and croutons; *Daumont*, mushrooms with a *dice*, or *salpicon*, of crayfish bound with *Sauce Nantua*, quenelles of fish forcemeat, slices of soft roes egged-and-bread-crumbed and fried; *Cardinal*, slices of lobster tails combined with slices of truffle.

I hope that the home cook, having mastered the simple classic sauces, will now be tempted to try some of these grander versions.

Shellfish offer an explosion of sensations for the eye and the palate as we enter the rococo haunts of the lobster, the crayfish, and the burrowing crab, the sandy lurking places of the scallop, the shrimp and the multitudinous cockle, and the seaweed-covered rocky retreats of the mussel.

LOBSTER

I suppose that for some people this blue-black grandee of the deep is an everyday dish. To me it is an increasingly rare feast, and stirs up memories of youthful extravagance. Those who do buy lobster will usually buy them freshly boiled, but shoppers who buy them live should kill them by sudden immersion in boiling water; this kills them instantly.

Cooking times: a lobster weighing 1 pound will be cooked after 15 minutes' boiling. For every additional 1 pound add 10 minutes.

ALAN
CRACKNELL

LOBSTER MORNAY

SERVES 4

two 1-pound freshly
boiled lobsters

3¾ cups Mornay sauce
(p. 33)

1 tablespoon Madeira,
muscatel, or port wine

1 teaspoon prepared
mustard

Split the lobsters into 4 half shells. Remove the black thread of intestine from the end of the tail and the sac from the head parts. Take the lobster meat out of the tails and claws and dice it. Now scoop out the soft and green edible parts from the heads and in a small bowl moisten them with the wine and the mustard and mix together thoroughly. Brush the lobster meat with this mixture. Next, put 2 tablespoons of the Mornay sauce into the bottom of each shell. Put the lobster meat back and cover with the rest of the sauce. Put under a hot broiler to brown. Ten minutes should be enough.

LOBSTER THERMIDOR

SERVES 4

two 1-pound freshly
boiled lobsters

1¼ cups Bercy sauce
(p. 25)

1½ cups béchamel sauce
(p. 19)

2 teaspoons prepared
mustard

Proceed as in the previous recipe, but do not dice the tail meat, which should be extracted whole, cut with a sharp knife into fine slices, and then put back, as if intact, into the shells, which have been previously moistened with a few tablespoons of the two sauces. Now crack the claws and extract the flaky meat and put it in a bowl with the green and soft parts scooped from the head. Add the mustard and mix all together well. Next, with a teaspoon, separate each slice of the tail meat and put in some of the mixture. Cover with the remaining sauces, thoroughly combined, and brown lightly under the grill.

Note: observe the differing use of mustard in this and the former recipe. In the first case the mustard is there simply to give a flavor. In the second, it is meant to sting a little.

LOBSTER IN COQUILLES

Although we cannot afford to eat lobster often, a lot can be done with one small lobster in mixed fish dishes, the best of which are coquilles: those served in shell-shaped dishes. The presence and flavor of lobster enhance a mix of small poached fillets of firm, nonoily fish, such as monk, sole, turbot. Covered in a good sauce, and put under the broiler or in a hot oven for a few minutes, coquilles make splendid lunch and supper dishes.

The deep conch shell of the scallop is best for these confections, in which the scallop itself can play a major part, as, of course, can mussels. Do ask the fishmonger for both shells of this beautiful bivalve; do not be content with the flat shell on which they are usually displayed. Deep scallop conch shells should be collected like fine china and kept as scrupulously clean and unchipped. (Besides, they are the prettiest of serving dishes, for a large number of poultry, meat, and vegetable dishes in general cookery.)

MIXED-FISH COQUILLE DISHES

These savory confections are useful in enabling the cook to make the most of small quantities of lobster (or crayfish or large prawns) by "stretching" them with other fish without obliterating the unique flavor and texture of those expensive crustacea. The selection of fish to be included will be guided by the cook's inclination and budget. The following recipe includes two different kinds of fish, apart from the lobster, and will give a flavor of lobster throughout.

COQUILLE OF LOBSTER TANANARIVE

SERVES 6

1 pound poached fillets of haddock (or whiting or flounder)

8 ounces poached monkfish or angler tail

1-pound lobster, cooked

1 1/4 cups heavy cream

2 teaspoons finely chopped chives

1 tablespoon ground green peppercorns

1 teaspoon creamed horseradish

1/2 teaspoon ground cloves

2 teaspoons muscatel or other sweet dessert wine

salt to season

1 1/2 pounds potatoes, cooked and mashed with 6 tablespoons butter and 1 whole egg with 1 egg yolk beaten into it

For serving

6 large scallop shells (or cocottes) 4 inches in diameter and 2 inches deep

Flake the haddock, cut up the monkfish into small pieces, and set both aside. Cut the lobster open, head to tail. Remove the black intestine and extract the inedible sac from the head. Spoon out from the head all the green and soft edible parts and put them into a mixing bowl. Set aside.

Extract all the flesh from the tail and claws. Cut up the tail meat into very fine slices and quarter these. Flake the claw meat and set all aside. Now pour the cream into the bowl containing the green and soft edible parts from the lobster head and beat together well. Add all the herbs and spices and the wine and blend together into a homogenous mixture.

Put 2 or 3 tablespoons of the mashed potato into the bottom of each scallop shell and pat down gently. On top of each, put 3 heaped tablespoons of the flaked and chopped fish and press it down flat. Add to each a tablespoon of the enriched thick cream and spread it over the fish. Add more potato, then more fish, and again more cream, and so on, until the flaked fish is all used.

The scallops should now be two-thirds full, and there should still be enough of the enriched cream to moisten all the lobster flesh, stirred around in it in the bowl. Distribute the lobster meat evenly in the 6 shells and press it down flat. The balance of the potato can now be put in to fill completely and make a mound on top of each shell. Put the shells on a baking sheet in the middle of a preheated 350°F oven for 20–25 minutes. Serve with a beurre blanc (p. 43) or a hollandaise sauce (p. 20).

COLD LOBSTER

Cook the lobsters, if bought live, as described on p. 54; split in half and clean as in Lobster Mornay (p. 56). Serve at room temperature, not chilled.

SAUCES FOR COLD LOBSTER

Most cold fish (and this is especially true of lobster, crayfish, prawns, and crab) lose much of their flavor when served at refrigerator temperature. It should be a rule therefore that, before serving such cold dishes, they should be allowed to reach at least a reasonable room temperature before they are brought to the table. The same rule applies to the mayonnaise and other sauces and the salads which accompany the fish.

These following sauces all go well with cold dishes of lobster and other shellfish.

Mayonnaise (p. 21) and all the sauces derived from it, the following being perhaps the most approved by custom and acclaim:

Remoulade sauce: into 1¼ cups mayonnaise work 1 teaspoon French mustard and 1 pounded anchovy fillet. Then fold in 2 teaspoons each of finely chopped pickled gherkin, parsley, capers, basil, and tarragon.

Escoffier mayonnaise: into 1¼ cups mayonnaise fold 1 teaspoon creamed horseradish and 1 teaspoon each of finely chopped parsley, chervil, and chives.

Tartare sauce: see p. 32.

Green sauce: to 1¼ cups mayonnaise, add 1 teaspoon of each of the following, all finely chopped and pounded: watercress, chervil, blanched young spinach leaf, fresh tarragon, and chives. (Fresh basil can be substituted for the tarragon to make a fresher-tasting sauce.)

These are the best-known mayonnaise sauces, but there remain many variants to be developed by the use of relishes, reduced to a spoonful or two of concentrated flavor, which can then be worked into the egg yolk before the oil is beaten in (p. 16).

Apart from mayonnaise, the sauce I recommend for frequent use is the gribiche (p. 31), made with hard-boiled egg yolks. Not to be despised for their simplicity are the range of vinaigrettes (p. 21).

CRAYFISH, SHRIMPS
SCAMPI (DUBLIN BAY PRAWNS)

The crayfish can be treated just like lobster, though it lacks the lovely claw meat of the latter. However, crayfish and all the other crustaceans mentioned above are expensive as the main ingredient of a meal. It is only good sense to combine very small quantities of these expensive fish with others to make mixed-fish dishes, such as pilafs, salads, soufflés, soups, and pies, where their pronounced individual flavors will still come through. Recipes of this nature will be found later in the book and will indicate the possibility for the home cook to economize while still occasionally indulging and—I hope—expanding his or her appreciation of the good things that come from the sea.

CRAB

Formerly, like the oyster, the mussel, and the scallop, one of the few privileges of the poor, the stereotyped dressed crab of the English "Margate" tradition provides splendid nutritional value. However, I believe it is still regarded as a holiday treat; part of periodical visits to the seaside, but not a regular feature in home menus. This is a pity because the Atlantic crab is better flavored and much meatier than those usually met with on the Mediterranean.

For those unfamiliar with the crab, the fish monger will willingly demonstrate how to open it and remove the few inedible parts. The cracking of the claws and the extraction of their meat takes a little time but is not unpleasant, and the dressing of the meat provides endless scope for happy experiment.

Cooking live crabs: If you buy live crabs, make sure the big claws are tied, to prevent any annoying nips as you get to them out of the bag when you get home. As with the lobster, the best way of killing a crab is to drop it quickly into a pan of boiling water. For crabs weighing between 1 and 2 pounds boil hard for 3 or 4 minutes and then simmer for 8 to 10 minutes more. Crabs weighing 2 pounds and over will require, after an initial rolling boil of 4 minutes, a further 12 to 14 minutes' simmering.

DRESSED CRAB

A crab of 1 to 1½ pounds is a very full and filling meal for one. This recipe, which departs from the English stereotype of crabmeat bulked out with bread crumbs and then sprinkled with vinegar, salt, and pepper, will be found to be something of an improvement.

SERVES 4

four 1-pound freshly cooked crabs

2½ cups thick béchamel sauce (p. 19)

4 tablespoons of a selected savory butter (p. 18 and below)

1 tablespoon finely chopped parsley

optional: fine bread crumbs, finely grated Parmesan, or other cheese sufficient to sprinkle thinly over each serving

For the savory butter

suggested ingredients, one of which is to be blended, in the quantities given, with 4 tablespoons butter:

1 teaspoon pounded garlic

2 teaspoons ground green peppercorns

2 small anchovy fillets, pounded

1 teaspoon prepared mustard

1 teaspoon creamed horseradish

1 teaspoon tomato paste

1 tablespoon finely chopped shallot

1 tablespoon finely chopped capers

1 tablespoon finely chopped celery heart

1 tablespoon finely chopped fennel

Break up the claws and legs of the crabs and extract all the white meat. Now tackle the intricately constructed, bony chine and extract the white meat from that. Put all the white meat together into one bowl.

Scoop out the brown meat and creamy substances from the shell. If it is summertime and one or two of the crabs is female, scoop out the lining of red coral from the large shell. Put all this meat, brown and red, into a separate bowl. Reserve and clean the crab shells.

Over a low heat, warm up the béchamel sauce, and add the savory butter of your choice. Stir well as the mingled sauce and butter become really hot. Do not allow to boil. Pour half of this combined mixture into a separate pan.

Put the brown and red meat into one of the pans, and the white meat into the other, in each case mixing the sauce and meat together. Now fill the clean crab shells with alternate tablespoonsful of white and dark meat till the saucepans are empty. Put on a baking sheet in a preheated 375°F oven for 10 minutes. Sprinkle with the parsley and serve.

Alternatively, at the penultimate stage, sprinkle the loaded shells with bread crumbs and Parmesan or other cheese and put in a hot 425°F oven for 6 minutes or until brown.

BOILED CRABS FOR A PARTY

Delicious as such sauced crab dishes are, a great deal of happiness can be had by simply placing an opened cooked crab, relieved of its inedibles, in front of each person at the table and providing whatever you have in the way of nutcrackers, lobster picks, marrow extractors, pickle forks, and skewers, as well as a sprinkler bottle containing a good relish (p. 16), paper napkins galore, bottles of good wine (red and or white), and fresh bread and butter.

Watch and listen as the claws go crack. Study the varying skills of the protagonists, particularly when they tackle the chine, which contains as much good meat as the claw, if only it can be skillfully extruded.

Perhaps this is the best way of all to eat crab; in a jolly company around the table, everyone busy and, in a sense, competitive, though there is no prize to be gained for being the first to exhaust one's crab's resources.

CRAB CURRY

This sauce, hot in both senses, can also be used with other crustacea and any firm fish.

SERVES 4

4 good crabs

For the curry sauce

1 small hot red chili, finely chopped

2 teaspoons finely grated gingerroot

2 teaspoons ground cumin

2 teaspoons powdered turmeric

2 teaspoons ground coriander

juice of 1 lemon

2 teaspoons wine vinegar

2 tablespoons Madeira, port, or full sherry

½ teaspoon cayenne pepper

1 teaspoon salt

Break off the claws of the crab and extract all the meat, both white and brown. Clean the main shells.

Blend all the ingredients for the sauce in a food processor, and then cook gently in a saucepan, stirring all the time, for 12–15 minutes. Distribute the sauce evenly in the crab shells. Mix the crabmeat together and lay it on top of the sauce. With two forks, turn the contents of the shells over, from the bottom up, so as to obtain a rough mixture of the two elements.

Cover the filled crab shells with foil and put into a moderate, 350°F oven for 15 minutes. Serve with cumin-and-clove-spiced long-grain rice and chopped tomatoes and onions.

MUSSELS

Within these black shells is to be found the concentrated essence and sea-impregnated succulence of seafood at its best. Even the oyster cannot compete—and the oyster is far less useful to the fish cook, losing much of its flavor when cooked. The mussel, on the other hand, improves with the slight cooking it should get: just enough to open it and to dress it. Mussels are excellent uncooked, but much better prepared and treated in their most popular and classic way as moules marinière, my next recipe.

Shopping note: when buying mussels, whether shaggy and barnacle-strewn or clean-shelled, buy a good many more than you estimate you will need. Experience indicates that at least one in ten shells will be open, broken, cracked, or filled with mud.

Preparation: scrub the shells well. Pull out the beard or byssus protruding from the center of the concave edge. Test each mussel by kneading strongly with the fingers. If any substance oozes out, discard. Reject those that are slightly open and do not immediately snap shut when you handle them.

MOULES MARINIÈRE

SERVES 4

3 pounds mussels	1 shallot, finely chopped
½ bottle white wine, not extremely dry	2 sprigs of fennel leaves
1¼ cups water	4 stalks and heads of parsley
1 teaspoon ground black pepper	¼ cup finely chopped parsley

Into a large two-handled lidded pan put the wine, water, pepper, shallot and sprigs of fennel and parsley. Reserve the chopped parsley. Load in the mussels as gently as possible. Shake them a little, to settle them down evenly. Cover and heat rapidly, to raise steam. Shake the pan and allow 30 seconds' further steaming before turning off the heat. Lift the lid, and give one more shake, then let the mussels, which will now all be open, stand for a minute, to allow their juices to drain down into the cooking liquid. With a large perforated spoon or ladle, transfer the mussels to a colander, placed over a bowl to collect any juices still draining from them. Cover with a cloth to keep warm. Now strain the cooking liquid into a smaller, more convenient pan. Add the mussel juices from the bowl under the colander and heat the liquid, but not to the boiling point. Stir in the chopped parsley and remove from the heat. Distribute the mussels in hot soup plates, and pour or ladle the hot liquid over them. One of the great flavors of the world.

VARIATION

Some people prefer a more substantial liquid, and, in another version of the recipe, the cooking liquid is thickened with beurre manié (p. 15) before stirring in the parsley and ladling over the mussels. To thicken 1¼ cups of liquid, use 1 tablespoon beurre manié made of equal proportions of butter and flour.

OTHER WAYS WITH MUSSELS

Once you have cleaned them and opened them by steaming, there are many ways of dressing mussels, all of them delicious. Put a small pat of any savory butter (p. 18) on each of a dozen mussels in the half shell and place them in a moderate oven for a few minutes. Again in the half shell, add a teaspoon of any sauce derived from the fish velouté or the béchamel and put under a hot broiler for a few minutes. And, vice versa, put a few mussels and the strained juices drained from them into any of the classic sauces, and it becomes miraculously transformed and improved. In this way mussels have played and still play a tremendous role in the history of fish cooking.

SCALLOPS

Several hundred years after Botticelli so beautifully depicted Venus arising in a scallop shell from the warm midland sea, another Italian, Maître Emilio Boscasso, chef of Hatchett's restaurant in Piccadilly, met a chilly end in the North Atlantic. On his way to benevolent internment in Canada with many other enemy aliens, his ship was torpedoed and sank with all hands.

The following recipe is by way of a tribute to a friend and one of the most resourceful of cooks.

SCALLOPS BOSCASSO

The recipe is a reminder of the ingenuity required to provide adequate meals at controlled prices in a climate of acute shortage. I am glad to reflect that Boscasso helped to raise the lowly scallop to the exalted status it now has in English cooking.

SERVES 4

4 large scallops or 8 small ones	2½ cups béchamel sauce (p. 19)
2 large potatoes, baked	4 tablespoons butter, melted
1 tablespoon olive oil	
1 shallot, finely chopped	5 cups court bouillon for nonoily fish (p. 28)
scant ¼ pound mushrooms, finely chopped	

Scoop out the potatoes leaving the skins intact. Brush the outsides of these very thinly with oil (or butter) and let them get crisp in a moderate oven. In the olive oil, in a small pan, cook the finely chopped shallot

and mushrooms until they almost form a puree. Add this mixture to the béchamel sauce.

Meanwhile remove the skirt (ragged edge) and the black, threadlike intestine from the scallops and poach them gently in the warm court bouillon for 3–4 minutes. Transfer them to a plate, reserving the orange "cock's combs" for garnish, and chop them up and keep them warm.

Now line the bottom of each potato skin with 2 tablespoons of the enriched béchamel sauce. Lay the chopped scallops over this. Pour over each some of the remaining béchamel sauce, leaving room for a layer of half the original contents of the potato skins, mashed, to be heaped on top. Brush the potato top—patterned with a fork—with melted butter and put in a hot oven to become a really deep brown. Sprinkle with parsley, and stick one "cock's comb" upright in the center of each half potato. To be consumed potato skins and all!

VARIATIONS

This simple recipe can be applied to all other poached fish and shellfish: lobster, sole, monkfish, or turbot Boscasso. The crisp potato skin is the feature of the dish; the sauce can be varied at the discretion of the cook.

OTHER SCALLOP SUGGESTIONS

Scallops go well with almost any sauce, particularly with Mornay (p. 33) or black butter (p. 25). Sliced horizontally and lightly fried *à la meunière*, they are delicious.

Although scallops are not quite so pungently reminiscent of the sea as mussels, they can be used to great effect in finishing a sauce or can be served sliced as a garnish for sole, turbot, halibut, brill, or monkfish. They are almost essential ingredients of a good fish pie (p. 89).

THE CEPHALOPODS

Octopus, squid, cuttlefish: comparative newcomers to the British scene, these are not only the most nourishing and subtly flavored of fish but, in the case of the squid and cuttlefish, are the easiest to cook of all the fish we have encountered so far. Their appearance may be intimidating, but they are quite easy to deal with.

The octopus is a tough customer and, unless he has been thoroughly beaten, will never really become tender, though the sauce that will come from him, and the vegetables and herbs cooked with him, will be exquisite; to be lapped up eagerly, with chunks of brown bread: a meal in itself. One fishmonger in the town where I live uses a small cement mixer, into which he shovels, along with three or four octopus, a couple of spadefuls of flint shingle from the beach, rotating it at full speed: the shingle breaks every sinew in the octopus in about 20 minutes. It is then ready to cook.

Such resources are not usually available to the home cook. When buying octopus, therefore, a shopper should inquire whether it has been already prepared for cooking. If the answer is yes, then why not have a go?

To clean a squid or cuttlefish: the best way to prepare these fish for cooking is to cut from the head to the tentacles—to be cooked with the rest of the fish—pull the head and any attachments away from the bag, remove the quill, in the case of the squid, or the chalky oval bone, in the cuttlefish (though these can be much more easily removed when the fish is cooked). Slit the bag at the apex of its closed end. Search for and remove any grit that you find there. The bag and the tentacles are all that are essential to cook, but the head should then be explored surgically to locate the ink sac, which will almost certainly, on a first occasion, disclose its presence only too clearly if it is broken into. This ink is an essential part of many recipes. Long familiarity with the squid and the cuttlefish has led me to confine my own preparations to making sure there is no grit lurking at the bottom of the closed end of the bag.

CUTTLEFISH CASSEROLE

This recipe can be used for squid and tenderized octopus as well, but in the case of octopus, cooking time should be extended to 1 hour, or until tender.

SERVES 4

1½ pounds cuttlefish	1 sprig of thyme
1½ cups finely chopped shallots	1 sprig of rosemary
¼ cup olive oil	3 bay leaves
1 cup chopped celery	1 pound tomatoes, peeled
¾ cup chopped green pepper	2½ cups red wine
a good pinch of ground allspice	about ½ cup tomato paste

Soften the shallots in the olive oil. Put in the cuttlefish, either cut up in pieces or whole. Move the fish around while it cooks for 12 minutes. Add the celery and the green pepper, and the herbs and spices. Cut up and lay the tomatoes over all and cook briskly until the tomatoes begin to meld with the other ingredients. Now transfer to an earthenware pot just big enough to hold all these ingredients along with the wine and the tomato paste, thinned with a spoonful or two of the wine. Cook in a preheated 350°F oven for about 40 minutes.

A SAUTÉ OF SQUID

SERVES 5

2 pounds squid, preferably small (with ink sacs and "quills" removed, see p. 64)	scant ⅔ cup olive oil
	salt and black pepper to taste
water	juice of ½ lemon
2 tablespoons wine vinegar	

Put the whole squid in a small pan. Add just enough water to cover and add the vinegar. Bring to the boil and simmer very gently for 45 minutes, or until tender. Remove from the heat. Drain, then cool under cold running water. Transfer to a plate and cut into small, 1-inch pieces or strips.

Heat the olive oil in a frying pan and gently sauté the squid pieces until very lightly browned. Remove from the oil to a hot dish. Season with salt and pepper and sprinkle with lemon juice. Serve with a dip of rouille (p. 86).

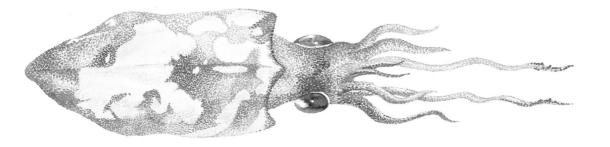

8

CURED &
PRESERVED FISH

In Britain we are fortunate to have a wide range of smoked, salted, and pickled fish, some prepared for centuries in these islands, others from northern Europe that we have come to know in recent years, readily available from the fishmonger or delicatessen. They range from the luxurious and expensive to simple everyday fare, and all make excellent eating.

Smoked salmon, trout, mackerel, and **eel,** are all best eaten as they are, with a squeeze of lemon juice or a sprinkle of a relish in which cayenne pepper is mildly present. Serve with them cress or cucumber sandwiches made with thin brown bread and butter.

Kippers are best broiled, brushed with butter and put to a high heat. Watch your kipper as it broils for the moment the main bone buckles and springs up, it is cooked. Whip it away onto a hot plate. Serve with toast and butter. (One should always remember that a single kipper never seems to be enough.)

The **bloater,** another and remarkable role played by that paragon of fishes, the herring, is as different from the kipper as Danish blue is from a good strong Cheddar. If you are lucky, you will find a hard roe inside; this, to me, is one of the great delicacies. Bake your bloater, unopened, in the oven (400°F) for 10 minutes. Accompaniments: as for kippers.

Smoked haddock is a marvelous exception to the rule that nonoily fish are not improved by smoking. (I have smoked gray mullet with some success, and I believe that large gray mullet are being smoked in the United States today.) There is no doubt that the fresh haddock, a quality fish when fresh, is immeasurably enhanced by smoking. (Smoked cod and whiting, though gallant challengers, are much better eaten fresh.)

To cook the smoked haddock, put it into a pan and cover with a half-and-half mixture of milk and water. Bring to the simmering point. Allow to cook gently for 3 minutes. Then withdraw the pan from the heat and allow the fish to complete its cooking in the hot liquid for 6 minutes more. Transfer to a dish and garnish generously with pats of butter. A recipe for kedgeree with haddock is on p. 90.

Arbroath smokies are small haddock. Brush well with butter and broil for a few minutes.

SOUSED HERRINGS OR MACKEREL

Soused herrings or mackerel are simple to prepare, and a wonderful cold food, accompanied by a potato-and-watercress salad.

SERVES 6

six 7-ounce fish, cleaned and headless

For the sousing liquid

wine vinegar

1 tablespoon pickling spice

1 teaspoon salt

1 large onion, finely sliced

2 bay leaves

Put the fish in the bottom of a baking dish large enough for them all to lie side by side. With a measuring cup, pour in water just to cover the fish, then pour in the same amount of wine vinegar, and put in all the other ingredients.

Place the dish in the middle of a 275°F oven and cook for 2 hours. Allow to cool, then put in the refrigerator, still in the sousing liquid, until you wish to serve.

PICKLED HERRINGS OR ROLLMOPS

SERVES 4

8 good-size herring fillets

For stuffing the fillets

2 pickled gherkins, finely chopped

2 shallots, finely sliced

4 teaspoons chopped capers

For the pickling mixture

2½ cups wine vinegar

1 tablespoon white vinegar

2 shallots, finely sliced

2 tablespoons salt

2 whole cloves

6 black peppercorns, crushed

1 large bay leaf

pinch of cayenne pepper

1 teaspoon sugar

Lay the fillets, skin down, on a flat surface, and cover them with the finely chopped gherkins, shallots, and capers. Roll each fillet up tightly, from the tail, and secure the bundles by spiking with half toothpicks. Lay the rollmops so that they fit tightly in a terrine. Pour over them the cold pickling liquid. Cover, and leave in the refrigerator for 4 days.

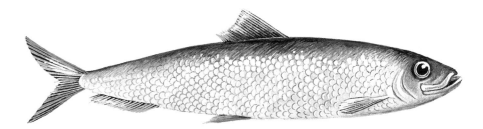

MACKEREL IN WHITE WINE

SERVES 4

4 small or 2 large mackerel	a few black peppercorns
½ bottle dry white wine	1 bay leaf
1¼ cups water	1 strip of lemon peel
2 onions, sliced	1 sprig of tarragon or a few celery leaves
salt to taste	chopped parsley

Make a court bouillon: put all the ingredients except the mackerel and parsley into a pan and bring to a boil. Cook steadily until the liquid is reduced by half. Allow to cool.

Clean the fish and put them in a pan. Strain the court bouillon over them and bring slowly to the simmering point. Simmer very gently for 5–8 minutes, depending on the size of the fish, then remove the pan from the heat and allow to cool.

Lift out the mackerel and remove the skin and bones. Place the fillets in a serving dish. Strain the cooking liquid and taste it. If the flavor is not strong enough, reduce the liquid a little more. When it is cool again, pour it over the fish.

The mackerel will keep, covered with foil, for several days in the refrigerator. Garnish with chopped parsley before serving.

MARINATED SARDINES

SERVES 6

2 pounds sardines	¼ cup court bouillon (p. 28) or water
flour	2 sprigs of thyme
salt to taste	2 bay leaves
scant ⅔ cup olive oil	peppercorns
4 cloves garlic, crushed	chopped parsley
scant ⅔ cup wine vinegar	
scant ⅔ cup dry white wine	

Clean the fish, but leave on their heads. Dust them with flour mixed with a little salt. Heat 4 tablespoons of the oil and fry the sardines until golden on both sides and cooked through. Remove the sardines to a serving dish and pour the remaining oil into the frying pan. Put in the garlic cloves and fry until they are golden, then add the vinegar, wine, court bouillon or water, herbs, peppercorns, and more salt. Boil fiercely for 4–5 minutes to reduce the liquid. Pour over the fish and allow to cool, then cover and refrigerate for at least 3 days. When you are ready to serve the sardines, bring the dish to room temperature, remove the thyme and bay leaves, and sprinkle with chopped parsley.

SEVICHE

The method of quick curing or pickling raw fresh salmon, as exemplified in the recipe for gravlax (p. 71), is simplified in the seviche. This is a recipe which may be applied to all the best firm fish, among which I would specifically select Dover sole, turbot, brill, halibut, bass, river trout, and—among the shellfish—the scallop, opened at home and immediately dealt with. Seviche is a dish which demands the very freshest of fine fish and calls for a piquant sweet-and-sour relish, as here, and an accompanying puree of vegetables or a potato salad.

SERVES 6

1½ pounds fillet, cut from a large fresh turbot	1 tablespoon finely chopped capers
For the marinade	2 teaspoons juice from a Spanish onion
1¼ cups lemon juice	
For the relish	2 small anchovy fillets, pounded
Scant ⅔ cup white wine vinegar	**For the garnish**
1 tablespoon muscatel or other dessert wine	black olives
	sprigs of parsley

With a sharp knife, cut the thick fillet into slices ⅛-inch thick and of roughly the same size and shape. Pass the slices, one by one, through a bowl containing the lemon juice, and lay them in a shallow dish, leaving a small space between each slice. When the bottom of the dish is covered, put a second layer of slices on top of the first, in much the same way as bricklayers lay bricks. Continue the process until all the slices are in the dish. Cover with the remaining lemon juice and put into the refrigerator for 6 hours.

Blend all the ingredients for the relish together, and allow to stand.

When the time comes, remove the fish from the refrigerator and, before serving, allow to stand for sufficient time to attain room temperature. Now drain off any extra lemon juice. Spoon over the relish and garnish with olives and parsley.

VARIATION

As an alternative to the sweet-and-sour relish with the seviche, try the mustard sauce which accompanies the gravlax (p. 71).

Incidentally, schnapps, aquavit, or vodka, in short nips, will be found to enliven the scene, though I myself prefer red wine.

GRAVLAX

This authentic Swedish recipe is only one of many variants and is a quick method of curing the salmon so that it is ready for eating only 12 hours after preparation. The sauce is an essential accompaniment.

SERVES 12

4½–5 pounds middle cut from a large fresh salmon

4–5 large bunches of dill

For the pickling mixture

3 tablespoons sea salt

3 tablespoons crushed white peppercorns

2 tablespoons superfine sugar

1 teaspoon saltpeter, available at pharmacies

For the sauce

6 tablespoons water

2 tablespoons prepared English mustard

2 teaspoons superfine sugar

1 tablespoon wine vinegar

scant 1 cup olive oil

1 tablespoon finely chopped dill

Blend all the ingredients for the pickling mixture together in a mortar; it is particularly important for the saltpeter to be distributed throughout. Scrape the skin of the salmon well, and fillet the fish from the ventral side without separating the two skinned sides when it is open. The filleting, if thorough, will produce many small channels into the salmon flesh. With your hands, rub the pickling mixture well into the exposed flesh. Bruise some bunches of dill and spread plenty of them over the fish. Now close the fish up, thus restoring the salmon to its original shape. Thickly line an oblong, straight-sided dish—one that is just big enough for the piece of salmon—with more bruised dill. Lay the salmon on this bed and pack more dill in around the edges, the amount of dill to be used being limited only by the amount that can be packed in. Cover the salmon with more dill and lay on it a board which will just fit into the top of the dish. Lay heavy weights on the board and put the dish in a cool larder for 12 hours (or, in summer, it can be placed at the bottom of the refrigerator).

Blend all the ingredients for the sauce together and put into a bowl.

To serve the salmon, remove it from the dish. Put it on a board. Open it out and brush off the excess dill and pickling mixture. Cut fine slices on the bias. Serve with the sauce and brown bread and butter as accompaniments.

9
SALADS

Most firm cooked fish, when cold, make excellent salads, and shellfish are especially suitable. This sort of casual though satisfying dish can be dressed either richly with a mayonnaise (p. 21) or one of its variations, such as tartare sauce (p. 32) or gribiche (p. 31), or very simply with a plain vinaigrette (p. 21).

Of the firm fish, salmon, turbot, tuna, sea bass, bream, and monkfish all make good Côte d'Azur-type salads, usually called Niçoise, but which greatly vary in composition. Canned salmon and tuna are, I think, at their best when served and eaten in this way. This recipe can be adapted to take account of the ingredients available.

Salade Niçoise

SERVES 4

1 pound of any of the fish named opposite, cut into small pieces

Other ingredients

¾ cup green beans, diced

4 small potatoes, diced

4 tomatoes, peeled and sliced

2 eggs, hard-boiled and coarsely chopped

8 small anchovy fillets

For the garnish

8 black olives

2 teaspoons each of finely chopped tarragon, basil, and chervil

---

Put the diced beans and potatoes into the middle of the salad dish and arrange the sliced tomatoes around the edge. Scatter the chopped eggs in the space between these two elements in the dish and cover them with the pieces of fish. Lay the anchovies on top of the fish so as to encircle the mound in the middle. Place the black olives, too, at intervals on top of the fish. Scatter the herbs over all, and sprinkle with a vinaigrette (p. 21).

Both fish and vegetables may be varied, substituting

cooked diced celeriac or cooked diced fennel bulb for the green beans, for example; but if the salad is to retain its character, it should always contain the tomatoes, the anchovies, and the olives. As to the layout of the different elements in the dish to make the best effect, everyone will have a personal idea of arrangement and decor.

A SEAFOOD SALAD

SERVES 6

6 cooked scallops	2 cucumbers, peeled and sliced lengthwise into 4-inch sticks
1 pound cooked and flaked fish (such as fresh haddock or whiting)	scant ⅔ cup aioli (p. 86)
1 tablespoon finely chopped parsley	6 medium-size tomatoes, peeled and halved horizontally
1 sweet red pepper, finely chopped	12 black olives, pitted
5 eggs, hard-boiled and very finely chopped	12 small new potatoes, cooked and halved
2 cups taramasalata (p. 86)	1 bunch of watercress
12 small artichoke bottoms, cooked	12 small radishes
	12 lemon quarters
1 large Romaine lettuce	1 large bowl of plain yogurt

Dice the scallops into small cubes. Mix with the flaked fish, lightly, in a bowl, together with the parsley and the sweet red pepper.

Mix the hard-boiled eggs thoroughly with the taramasalata. Fill the artichoke bottoms with this mixture, which should be thick enough to be heaped up in mounds.

Cut the lettuce into fine strips and fluff it up into a chiffonade.

Select a large circular dish and arrange the elements on it as follows. With the cucumber sticks, make a reserve in the center of the dish, into which ladle the diced scallops and flaked fish. Spoon the aioli carefully onto this fish mixture. Surround this reserve with the halved tomatoes, with an olive pressed into the center of each. Now place the filled artichoke bottoms around the ring of tomatoes. Surround these concentric circles with the shredded lettuce, on which distribute the potato halves. Fill the interstices of this display with small sprigs of watercress, radishes, and quarters of lemon. Serve with a bowl of yogurt and with hot French bread and a strong red wine.

VARIATIONS

This is an obviously expandable recipe, which, with the addition of other seafood, sauces, and dips, can soon become a considerable buffet or indeed a banquet. Consider the possibilities offered by half small lobsters, sliced, brushed with tartare sauce (p. 32) and laid, in the half shells, among the lettuce. Prawns; crayfish; dressed crabs; mussels; purees of vegetables, such as carrots, Jerusalem artichokes, mushrooms: all can have their place. The only limitation is the cook's budget.

MIXED FISH SALAD

SERVES 4

3 scallops, poached and diced

4 large shrimp, cooked peeled and halved lengthwise

1 pound of any firm cooked fish, such as monkfish, sea bass, or bream, cut into small pieces

1 large bunch of watercress

1 large carrot, cooked and shredded

1 tablespoon finely chopped parsley

For the vinaigrette

½ clove garlic, crushed

1 teaspoon sugar

½ teaspoon salt

1 teaspoon prepared English mustard

1 tablespoon chopped shallots

1 tablespoon chopped chives

3 tablespoons wine vinegar

scant ⅔ cup olive oil

Scatter the watercress over the salad dish. Mix all the pieces of fish and shellfish together in a bowl, and distribute them over the watercress. Sprinkle with the shredded carrot, then the parsley.

For the vinaigrette, pound all the ingredients, except the oil, with the vinegar. Now pour in the olive oil and beat well together to amalgamate. Distribute the dressing carefully over the salad so that all the fish is covered.

In the above recipe, both the fish and the vinaigrette are variable.

RATATOUILLE AND FISH SALAD

The Provençal ragout, the ratatouille (p. 39), may be dressed with vinaigrette and served cold. It then makes an excellent salad to serve with cold shellfish or other firm fish.

10
SOUPS

VELOUTÉ OF BRILL

Fish soups based on velouté and béchamel sauce should be a priority in the home kitchen. These soups are velvet-smooth, rich, and nutritious and make complete meals in themselves. This recipe can be made with all nonoily fish.

SERVES 4

8-ounce fillet of brill	*scant ⅔ cup light cream*
3¾ cups fish stock (p. 30)	*4 tablespoons butter*
	1 tablespoon white wine
2½ cups fish velouté sauce (p. 20)	*salt and pepper*
	For the garnish
2 egg yolks	*watercress butter (p. 18)*

Poach the fish in the stock for 3–4 minutes. Remove and pound it to a puree, then set aside. Strain the stock, and add the velouté sauce to it. Raise the heat and allow to simmer while stirring for 5–6 minutes. Remove from heat and stir in the puree of fish. Pass through a fine sieve. Return to the pan and bring to the simmering point. After a few minutes, remove from the heat, and allow to cool a little. Add the egg yolks, thoroughly beaten with the cream and a few tablespoons of the hot liquid. Stir all well together. Now work in the butter in small pieces. Heat the soup up to the simmering point again and allow it to simmer very gently for a few minutes only. Add the wine and taste for seasoning with salt and pepper. Serve with watercress butter as a garnish.

VELOUTÉ OF MUSSELS

This is a velouté soup of the first distinction. Follow the previous recipe, but substitute for the fish stock 3¾ cups of the liquid in which mussels have been cooked (see moules marinière, p. 62). Add this to the velouté sauce, which, for this particular occasion, has been made with a fish stock strongly flavored with leeks. Complete the process of thickening with egg yolks, cream, and butter. Serve 4 or 5 poached mussels as garnish to each plate of soup. A grander version of this soup can be made by adding a puree of mussels themselves to the velouté. Serve with a parsley or fennel butter (p. 18).

FISH AVGOLEMONO SOUP

This soup is a simple, delicious, and nourishing variant on a classic Greek dish.

SERVES 6–7

1 pound fillets of whiting, cod, hake, or haddock

2¼ quarts rich fish stock (p. 30)

6 tablespoons long-grain rice

2 eggs

1 tablespoon medium-dry white wine

juice of 2 lemons

pepper and salt to taste

2 tablespoons finely chopped parsley

Poach the whiting in the stock for 6 or 7 minutes. Remove from the stock to a dish and cut into small (½-ounce) pieces. Set aside to cool. Now put the rice into the stock and cook quickly until tender. Remove from the heat to cool down. Meanwhile beat the eggs, wine, and lemon juice together. Add to this a ladleful of the stock and beat well. Incorporate this mixture into the body of the stock. Add the pieces of whiting. Season with pepper and salt. Replace the soup on the heat and make piping hot but without allowing it to boil. At the last moment, just before serving, shower in the parsley. Ladle into very hot soup bowls and serve at once.

Note: the rich fish stock for this soup should include in its making a small red mullet and some small portions of cuttlefish, octopus, or squid. The final excellence of the soup greatly depends on this enrichment of the stock.

CRAB AND LEEK SOUP

One of my favorite béchamel-based soups, this recipe can be made with other nonoily fish and shellfish.

SERVES 4

1 medium-size crab, freshly cooked

the white of 4 leeks, finely chopped

4 or 5 sprigs and stalks of parsley

scant ⅔ cup white wine

a pinch of black pepper

a pinch of cayenne pepper

salt

3¼ cups water

3¾ cups béchamel sauce (p. 19)

4 tablespoons parsley butter (p. 18)

2 teaspoons chopped chives

lemon quarters

Break open and extract all the white and brown meat from the crab. Keep them separate and set aside.

Make a vegetable stock with the leeks, parsley, wine, peppers, salt, and water. Boil this until it has reduced to 2½ cups. Mash the brown crab meat with a wooden spoon until smooth, and blend it with the béchamel over low heat.

Loosen the mixture with the strained prepared stock and simmer gently for 5 minutes. Season to taste and fold in all the flaked white crab meat.

Ladle the soup into hot soup bowls. Add a pat of parsley butter and a sprinkle of chives to each bowl.

Serve with lemon quarters and brown bread and butter.

SHRIMP BISQUE

The bisque is an excellent soup based on a foundation of small quantities of rice cooked to a smooth paste.

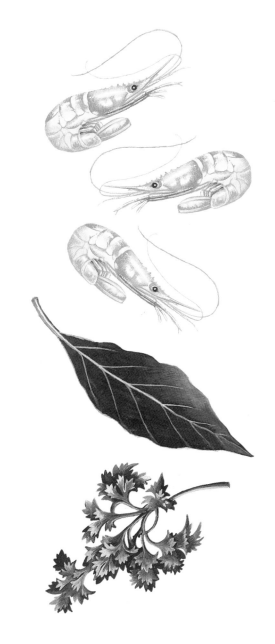

SERVES 4

1¼ cups water	pinch of saffron
1¼ cups milk	3¾ cups light cream
1 pound fresh shrimp	1 tablespoon finely chopped parsley
1 tablespoon sweet rice	
1 bay leaf	salt and pepper to taste
1¼ cups white wine	

Put the mixture of milk and water into a saucepan and bring briskly to a boil. Wash the shrimp thoroughly. Throw them in and cook for 2 minutes. Lift them out with a perforated spoon and put them aside on a plate to cool.

Strain the milk-and-water mixture into another pan. Add the rice and bay leaf and allow to cook steadily as you shell the shrimp, leaving 4–5 of the larger ones unshelled. After cooking for 30 minutes, the rice will have begun to break up and the liquid to thicken. Put the peeled shrimp into a blender with 6 tablespoons of the liquid and reduce to a thick puree. Return the puree to the pan. Add the wine, bring to the simmering point, and cook for 6–7 minutes.

Infuse the saffron in a tablespoon of the hot liquid and stir this into the soup. At this penultimate stage, chop up the unpeeled shrimp and blend them with their shells, into a puree, with half the cream. Pass this through a fine sieve into the soup. Now stir in the rest of the cream and the finely chopped parsley.

Note: a teaspoon of rouille or aioli (p. 86) provides a startling contrast in flavor, which is exciting with this kind of soup. Crayfish, scampi, and crab also make fine rice-based bisques.

HAMPSTEAD HOTPOT

To make this fish stew, a fish kettle or an asparagus kettle with a draining tray is the best pan to use. If you don't have one, the tray of a pressure cooker and a large saucepan could be used instead.

SERVES 6

⅔ cup olive oil

4 shallots, roughly chopped

2 cloves garlic, chopped

1 pound tomatoes, peeled and chopped

2 quarts boiling water

⅔ cup white wine

½ pound whiting or dab, cut into small pieces

¾ pound squid, cut into small pieces

½ pound monkfish tail fillet

2 small red mullet

8 medium shrimp, uncooked

pinch of saffron or powdered turmeric

salt, cayenne and black peppers to season

Remove the draining tray from the kettle at the start of the operation. Heat the oil in the bottom of the kettle. Add the shallots and garlic and cook until they are soft. Add the tomatoes and continue to cook, mashing with a wooden spoon, until they have combined with the oil to form a puree. Pour in the boiling water and the white wine, and add the whiting or dab and the squid. Cook steadily for 20 minutes.

Now replace the draining tray in the kettle with the monkfish laid on it and poach for 10 minutes. Add the red mullet and shrimp and cook gently for 8 minutes more. Remove the kettle from the heat and let it stand for 2 minutes. Lift the tray and transfer the monkfish, mullet, and shrimp to a hot dish. Replace the kettle on the heat and boil briskly. Add the saffron, salt, and the peppers, and cook until the dab or whiting has disintegrated.

Meanwhile, cut the monkfish into small pieces, fillet the mullet, and shell the shrimp. Immerse them on the tray in the kettle, not to cook further but simply to heat. Remove the tray once more. Put the fish into a deep, hot dish. Ladle the boiling soup into hot bowls through a wide-meshed strainer, and add 2 teaspoons of aioli (p. 86) to each bowl. Serve with thick slices of toasted French bread.

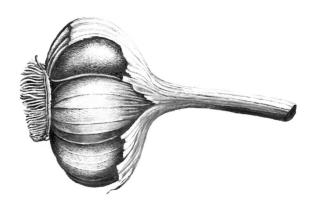

WATERZOOI

Waterzooi is a Belgian dish, usually made with freshwater fish—perch is particularly good—but firm-fleshed sea fish such as monkfish, angelfish, and turbot all make excellent waterzooi, as does the brill I have chosen here. Use flounder if brill is unavailable.

SERVES 4

2 pounds brill	2 sprigs of thyme
1 carrot	1 bay leaf
1 leek	salt and pepper
3 stalks celery	pinch of ground nutmeg
4 tablespoons butter	juice of ½ lemon
4 shallots, finely chopped	¼ cup heavy cream
scant ⅔ cup dry white wine	(optional)
scant 2 cups rich fish stock (p. 30)	

Clean the carrot, leek, and celery and cut them into thin julienne strips. Melt the butter in a large pan, put in the shallots and other vegetables, and cook gently until they are soft. Do not let them brown.

Cut the brill into pieces weighing about 2 ounces and put them on top of the vegetables. Pour the wine and stock over the fish, put in the thyme and bay leaf, and season with salt, pepper, and nutmeg.

Bring the contents of the pan to a boil, then lower the heat as far as possible, cover the pan, and simmer gently for 10 minutes. There should be barely a bubble on the surface of the liquid.

Remove the fish to a warm tureen and keep warm. Stir the lemon juice into the cooking liquid and remove the thyme and bay leaf. Heat through, and if you are using cream, stir it in now. Pour the stock over the fish and serve the stew in soup plates. Plain boiled potatoes go well with it.

DUTCH MUSSEL SOUP

SERVES 4–5

2 pounds small mussels	1 thick slice celeriac, diced
½ bottle white wine	scant 4½ cups water
4 tablespoons butter	salt and pepper
1 large onion, chopped	1 stalk celery, very finely chopped
2 leeks, sliced	
1 carrot, diced	

Clean the mussels thoroughly (see p. 61) and discard any that will not close (or that feel too heavy). Put them into a large pan with the wine, cover, and steam for a few minutes until the mussels open. Shake the pan from time to time. Remove the mussels from the pan, and when they are cool enough to handle, take them out of their shells and set aside. Discard any mussels that do not open. Pour any liquid from them back into the pan and strain all the cooking liquid through a muslin-lined sieve.

Melt the butter in a large heavy-bottomed pan and gently cook the onion, leeks, carrot, and celeriac for 15 minutes. Do not let them brown. Add the water, the mussel liquid, a little salt and pepper, and simmer for 20 minutes.

Add the finely chopped celery and simmer for 5 minutes more. Return the mussels to the soup, heat through, and serve hot.

—11—
MISCELLANEOUS FISH DISHES

In this chapter I have gathered a wide range of dishes—terrines, pâtés and mousses, pies and pilafs, quenelles, fish cakes, and soufflés. In each case I have given one or two recipes to serve as patterns. They can be varied according to the fish available.

TERRINES

Fish terrines are simple dishes to make and can be much varied in flavor and texture. Basically they should combine a stiff puree of supporting fish, such as whiting, flounder, or lemon sole, enriched by shellfish for flavor, with small whole fillets of a fine firm fish, such as Dover sole, brill, John Dory, turbot, or halibut, to give body. These fillets are distributed evenly throughout the mixture, and the whole pressed down into a terrine, covered, and cooked slowly in the oven in a bain-marie. The only binding agent required for the puree is a minimum of egg, butter, and heavy cream. Terrines may also combine a puree of fish and a puree of green vegetables to give a contrast of color and taste. Whole fillets of fish may be used to line the dish and wrap around the forcemeat. They may be served cold, but not chilled, with a mayonnaise-based sauce (see p. 58), or hot.

TERRINE OF DOVER SOLE WITH SHRIMP

SERVES 6

1 pound fillets of whiting, lemon sole, or flounder	½ teaspoon salt
¼ pound cooked and peeled shrimp	pinch of cayenne pepper
4 large scallops, cleaned	4 tablespoons butter
1 large egg	1 pound fillets of Dover sole, cut into roughly 1-ounce pieces
½ cup heavy cream	
1 teaspoon powdered turmeric	

Pass the whiting, shrimp and scallops through a blender. Put the mixture into a bowl and with a wooden spoon, fold in the egg and cream, previously lightly beaten together. Season with turmeric, salt, and cayenne and work the butter in well.